Lincolnshire People

Volume 2

Compiled and Edited by John R. Ketteringham

Published by Lincolnshire Books

First published in Great Britain by Lincolnshire Books

ISBN: 187237512X

Also by the author

The Church that moved(1983)

Lincoln Cathedral : A History of the Bells (1987)

A Lincolnshire Hotchpotch (1989)

A Second Lincolnshire Hotchpotch (1990)

Lincolnshire People (1995)

James Arundel of Locksley Hall, North Somercotes (1995)
A Cathedral Miscellany (1997)

Designed, typeset and produced for the publishers
by Peter Taylor, Aardvark Art.

Printed by G.W. Belton Ltd., Gainsborough, Lincs

LINCOLNSHIRE BOOKS
Official publishers to Lincolnshire County Council
County Offices
Newland
Lincoln LN1 1YL

CONTENTS

CONTENTS (CONTINUED)

FOREWORD

There are already books on Lincolnshire history and folklore, on the buildings and monuments and on some of Lincolnshire's better known sons, but I believe that Dr John Ketteringham's book on the lives of Lincolnshire Women is the first devoted entirely to the "fair sex". It tells of women from different times and backgrounds who have made their mark on the history of this County, in a variety of ways, over the ages.

These women must be admired for their ideals, achievements and determination. Most lived in an age when it was considered that a woman's place was in the home, bringing up a large family and being a dutiful wife to an often selfish and boorish husband!

I invite you to read this book and discover for yourselves the lives of the famous, the infamous and those Women of Lincolnshire who, for better or worse, have carved a name for themselves in Lincolnshire history. You will not be disappointed.

Bridget Cracroft-Eley
H M Lord Lieutenant for Lincolnshire

Dedicated to all those ladies who have helped in their many ways to put the 'forgotten county' on the map.

PREFACE AND ACKNOWLEDGEMENTS

It was with some trepidation that I accepted the invitation to compile a book on *Lincolnshire Women*.

I thought it would probably be rather a thin volume because, until the late nineteenth century, women were expected to remain at home and few reached prominence outside their immediate family circle.

There were, of course, exceptions but not enough to make a book of this nature an attractive project. However, as I investigated and made it known that I was undertaking this task I received many useful suggestions and, in fact, it has been a most interesting and rewarding undertaking.

Of the fifty-six ladies included herein nineteen are still living and I am grateful to them all for their interest and co-operation. I am also grateful to agents and others who have spared the time to read through my drafts and make corrections and suggestions.

As will be seen from the Table of Contents the book includes ladies from all walks of life and many occupations. I could not possibly pretend to have sufficient knowledge to write about opera and concert singers, sports people, explorers, actresses and authors. I am, therefore, very grateful to those with expert knowledge who have read articles on particular individuals. I have not mentioned by name all who have helped but feel I must particularly mention my wife, who has read every article and made many useful suggestions, and Ruth Tinley who has also read the whole manuscript and brought an independent viewpoint as well as making a number of suggestions.

At the end of the day, of course, the decision on who to include and who to omit and any errors are my own. I acknowledge with gratitude the assistance of the librarians at Lincoln Central Library, Lincolnshire Library Headquarters, Grimsby Central Library and Bishop Grossteste College. I am grateful for permission to quote from articles or to use articles in full as detailed in the footnotes to the particular article.

I acknowledge the interest of Lincolnshire Books whose decision to publish *Lincolnshire Women* enabled me to meet so many interesting ladies and I also thank Lincoln Soroptimists for their interest.

John R. Ketteringham
June 1998

Elisabeth ALLAN

Actress

Elizabeth Allan was born in Skegness on 9 April 1908 and was the youngest of five children of Alexander and Amelia Allan. Her father was a local doctor and Elizabeth was educated at Polam Hall a Quaker School in Darlington. After leaving school Elizabeth taught in a kindergarten for a short period before overcoming parental opposition to take up a career on the stage. She won a scholarship to the Old Vic training school and her first appearance on the stage was a walk-on part at the Lyric Hammersmith in September 1927 during an Old Vic production of *The Taming of the Shrew*. Her first speaking part was in the following March in *The School for Scandal* and soon after she went on tour with Ben Greet's Shakespearean repertory company.

Elizabeth made her West End debut at St. James's Theatre on 1 February, 1930 in A. A. Milne's *Michael and Mary* and this was the turning point in her career. In September 1932 she again went on tour before leaving the stage to appear in films.

Her first film appearance was in *Alibi* released in September 1931 and she appeared in several other films before appearing in the supporting role in *Michael and Mary* which was released in 1932. She was then co-starred with Ivor Novello in *The Lodger* and she also had a part in *Service for Ladies* which starred Leslie Howard. On 6 June, 1933 Elizabeth married her agent Captain Bill O'Bryan, M.C. and in the same year she was put under contract by M. G. M. and went to Hollywood. In 1934 she costarred with Robert Montgomery in *The Mystery of Mr X* and in the following year she played Mrs Copperfield in M.G.M's film of *David Copperfield* which had a star-studded cast including W.C. Fields, Freddie Bartholomew, Frank Lawton, Basil Rathbone and Lionel Barrymore.

Other notable films followed but in 1937 Elizabeth returned to England and resumed her stage career. She appeared in many plays throughout the 1940s and 1950s and her last stage appearance was in September 1958 at the Grand Theatre, Leeds in *These People, Those Books*. During the 1940s she appeared in three films made by Ealing and one each by London Films and Columbia. In 1953 Elizabeth starred in two British Lion films; *The Heart of the Matter* with Trevor Howard and with Jack Hawkins in *Front Page Story*.

In 1951 Elizabeth Allan made her first appearance on television when she became a member for about eighteen months of the panel of the BBC game *What's My Line*? Fellow member of the panel, Gilbert Harding, who was not renowned for his chivalry commented that she was one of the nicest women he had ever worked with. Praise indeed coming from Gilbert! In April 1959 she helped to devise *Swop Shop* in which she took part and Elizabeth and her husband were directors of Television Advisory Services Ltd. In December 1970 Elizabeth Allan left public life and resided in Hove, Sussex becoming very involved with an organisation for disabled men. She died on 27 July 1990 at the age of 82.

Anne ASKEW

Martyr

One of the bravest of Lincolnshire women, Anne Askew, was born at Stallingborough in 1521 and was the daughter of Sir William Askew or Ascough. Anne was highly educated and a serious student of the bible who was able to form her own opinions seeing both the rights and wrongs of traditional religious beliefs. She was prepared to fight against these wrongs, as many of the clergy of Lincoln Cathedral found when they tried to argue with her.

A marriage was arranged for Anne's eldest sister to Thomas Kyme of Friskney but the bride-to-be died and to avoid financial loss Anne was offered as substitute. Although she bore her husband two children, Anne eventually left him to go to London. It has been said that her brother Francis, whose monument is to be seen in Stallingborough church, betrayed her religious principles and she was in danger of arrest, but it may be that her religious views so offended the local clergy that she was forced to join other Protestant reformers in London.

London was torn apart by religious discord and Anne spoke out boldly against transubstantiation and other dogmas of the old faith. She was in communication with many ladies of the Court including Catherine Parr, the sixth and last wife of Henry VIII, who was an active supporter of reform.

Anne was charged with heresy and in March 1545 she appeared before the Lord Mayor of London and the infamous Bishop Bonner who is said to have sent two hundred Protestants to the stake. Anne was not intimidated and the Bishop tried to befriend her but she would not be persuaded and all attempts to make her deny her beliefs failed. She continued to preach against the establishment and within a year she had been arrested and indicted again for heresy. This time there was no escape and she was committed to Newgate and given a final chance to recant. She refused and was moved to the Tower where she was questioned about her association with Catherine Parr. Torturing failed to obtain a confession and such was her condition after this ordeal that she had to be carried to the stake at Smithfield. Even while the flames were inflicting more pain on her she contradicted the Catholic prayers being read by the clergy. Anne was aged twenty-five when she died in 1546.

The manner of burning Anne Askew, Iohn Lacels, Iohn Adams, & Nicolas Belenian, with certane of ye counsell sitting in Smithfield.

FURTHER READING
Wilson, D. *Tudor Tapestry* (1972)

Annie BESANT

Political Campaigner

Soon after Annie Besant came to live at Sibsey with her husband an incident took place which changed her life and gave the world a most remarkable lady.

Annie was actually born on 1 October 1847 in London and was the daughter of William and Emily Page. She was educated privately in England, Germany and France. Her early education was in the home of a family friend, Miss Ellen Marryat, whose small school was not typical of the time. Miss Marryat did not believe in learning by heart and taught her pupils to write about things which interested them but above all she expected her pupils to think for themselves. She went on to private schools in Germany and France and, at the age of sixteen Annie, who was unusually well educated for a girl at that time, returned home. After an engagement of two years she married Frank Besant.

Frank had very high ideals of a husband's authority but Anne was intelligent, proud and quite hot tempered so clashes with her husband were inevitable. They moved to Cheltenham where Frank had a teaching post but Annie wasn't interested in housekeeping and she started writing short stories which were published. Two children were born, a son Digby, in 1869 and a daughter, Mabel in 1870.

After their move to Sibsey in 1871, although Annie found the church and vicarage beautiful, she was very lonely. One day she was alone in the church and decided to give an impromptu sermon. The feeling of power which this gave her was the foundation of her remarkable career as a public speaker. In 1873 Annie and her husband separated; a rare move at that time. They agreed that Digby would remain with his father and Mabel with her mother. Although Frank made an allowance of a quarter of his salary to Annie she had to find what work she could in order to support herself and her daughter.

Space precludes a full discussion of "the many lives of Annie Besant" as one biographer puts it. She fought for justice in almost every area of life : marriage, working conditions, law, science, religion, motherhood, birth control, poverty, education and politics.

In 1933 Annie Besant died in Madras at the age of eighty-five.

FURTHER READING

Nethercott. A. The First Five Lives of Annie Besant (1960)

The Last Four Lives of Annie Besant (1963)

Priscilla BIGGADIKE

Murderess

On 30 September 1868 Richard Biggadike of Stickney returned home from work and, after having his tea, became violently ill. His wife, Priscilla, told the doctor that Richard had only consumed the same food that herself, the three children and the two lodgers had taken. Richard died at six o'clock the next morning and an autopsy found traces of a large amount of arsenic.

Priscilla suggested that her husband had committed suicide but she was arrested for murder together with one of the lodgers, Thomas Proctor who was suspected of being her lover. At the trial in Lincoln on 11 December 1868 it was agreed that there was not enough evidence against Proctor. Priscilla was sentenced to death and the sentence was carried out at Lincoln on 28 December 1868. She was the first woman to be executed inside a prison after public executions ended.

SOURCE
Lincoln, Rutland and Stamford Mercury 18 December 1868

Shirley BLOOMER

Tennis Champion

Shirley Bloomer had the pedigree to succeed at sport. Her parents, Bill and Kathleen Bloomer, were both scratch golfers and were county standard also at a number of games. Born in Grimsby on 13 June 1934, Shirley and her brother, Robin, were encouraged to try a variety of sports.

As a child Shirley was an "all-rounder" and she says "I suppose I would not have been successful later at sport had it not been for my brother. Robin was four years older, and, provided I could play to a decent standard, I was allowed to join in with him and his friends. At five I could throw well over arm and had an over arm service of sorts!"

At the age of twelve Shirley won the Lincolnshire Eighteen and Under Girls' Tennis Championship and she was selected for a special coaching session with Hazel Wightman, the American donor of the Wightman Cup. This was an annual team competition between the U.S.A and Britain. After the coaching session Shirley was invited to Wimbledon to watch the competition. Most of the matches provided easy victories for the United States and Shirley realised that getting to the top of British sport, particularly tennis, need not count for much when it came to World standards. Some ten years later, in 1957, Shirley was the French Open Champion, the No. 1 woman in Europe, World No. 3 and British No. 1. She had put Grimsby and Lincolnshire on the tennis map.

For part of the war Shirley and her family were evacuated but on returning to Grimsby she played tennis on her grandmother's court and at Grimsby Tennis Club. She received considerable encouragement and Shirley appreciated the amount of time that Grimsby tennis players spent practising with her.

At the age of thirteen Shirley left Grimsby to continue her education at Sherborne School for Girls in Dorset. 'Fuz' Dewhurst, a former Wimbledon player, was in charge of tennis coaching and proved to be an outstanding coach who guided Shirley throughout her career. 'Fuz' had to convince Shirley that she must cease to consider herself an all-rounder and concentrate on tennis if she wanted to be successful. This was not an easy decision as she was playing for Dorset Juniors at hockey and lacrosse and had won the National 16 and Under Squash title as well as the National Schoolgirls tennis championship at the Queen's Club.

With a year to spare before University, Shirley decided to give herself a chance on the tennis circuit. Her results surprised her and were good enough to be accepted for Wimbledon. The game was still amateur at the start of the 1950s but soon expenses paid invitations came her way. Not surprisingly, the University place was never taken up!

Shirley competed in the Wimbledon Singles nineteen times between 1952

and 1974 and she was a Singles quarter finalist in 1956 and 1958. She was a Wimbledon finalist in the Ladies Doubles with Pat Ward in 1955 and a semi-finalist in the USA Open Singles in 1956. Shirley's best year was 1957 when she was French Open Champion and also winner of the British Hard Court and Italian championships. In 1958 she was a finalist in the French Open winning the Mixed Doubles title.

Shirley was ranked in the world's top ten women from 1955 to 1958; a period when British women's tennis was at its post war best. She played in the British winning Wightman Cup Teams in 1958 and 1960 with which included Angela Mortimer, Christine Truman and Ann Jones all of whom were major championship winners.

In 1959, Shirley married Christopher Brasher, the 1956 Melbourne Olympic Steeplechase Gold Medalist. Their three children, two girls and a boy, are keen on sport. Shirley has remained close to tennis, writing freelance for magazines and was Lawn Tennis Correspondent for the *Observer* for several years. As a part-time coach she has helped more than twenty-five National Junior tennis title winners. Her former pupils include Lesley Charles, finalist in the Wimbledon mixed doubles; Jeremy Bates, Davies Cup player and Wimbledon Mixed Doubles Champion; Federation Cup players Sam Smith and Karen Cross as well as former British No. 1, Lizzie Jelfs.

After her marriage Shirley lived in Chelsea and then in Petersham, Surrey, but her links with Grimsby remain through her brother, a solicitor who has always lived and practiced there. During her tennis career she could rarely forget Grimsby, for the trawler men followed her results and wrote to her. She found it odd that '...they wrote to me, but I've always admired the toughness and bravery of those who go to sea to earn their living. In top class sport real danger is not often present but you do need to be quite tough and mentally brave. Being born in Grimsby, maybe, some of the 'trawling' qualities rubbed off on me and helped my tennis!

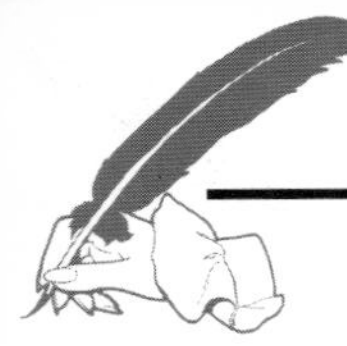

Enid BLYTON

Authoress

The Blyton family, who were ancestors of the children's author, Enid Blyton, were farmers in Lincolnshire for several centuries before George Blyton broke the mould and became a cordwainer (shoemaker). He was a Methodist Local Preacher and it was said that his main ambition was to go to the Fiji Islands to convert the heathen. Instead, he remained at home in Swinderby making fine boots and shoes and raising a large family. He did, however, name his youngest son, Thomas Carey Blyton in honour of Thomas Carey who was one of the founders of the Baptist Missionary Society. Thomas eventually left Swinderby to become a linen draper in Sheffield and he married Mary Ann Hanly in Camberwell in 1864.

Thomas Carey, junior, was born in 1870 and was the fourth of Mary Ann's seven children. He was a salesman with a cutlery firm in Sheffield but he had a great thirst for knowledge. Thomas studied astronomy, teaching himself French, German and shorthand. He also learned to play the piano and banjo, painted in water colours, was a good photographer, wrote poetry and was a great reader. In 1896 he married Theresa Mary Harrison and it was on 11 August 1897 after they had moved to London with his firm that their first child Enid Mary was born. As a young child Enid visited her grandparents and her cousins recalled playing with her at Swinderby.

The marriage of Thomas and Theresa was not a happy one and shortly before Enid's thirteenth birthday her father left his wife and children to start a completely new life without them. Enid had been greatly influenced by her father and the shock of his departure was very great.

When Enid was fifteen she entered a children's poetry competition run by Arthur Mee who liked her verses and asked to see more of her work. Enid continued with her writing when time permitted and had several poems published particularly in *Nash's Magazine*.

On 28 August 1924 Enid Blyton married Hugh Pollock who she had met after he joined the firm of George Newnes as a editor of the book department. She was now able to devote more time to her writing and in 1924 Newnes published *The Enid Blyton Book of Fairies* and in the following year *The Enid Blyton Book of Bunnies*. Many other books followed but it was not until 1942 that the first of the Famous Five books appeared entitled *Five on a Desert Island*. The second, *Five Go Adventuring* appeared in the following year. Hugh and Enid's daughter Gillian Mary was born on 15 July 1931 and a second daughter, Imogen Mary was born on 27 October 1937. Unfortunately Hugh and Enid divorced in December 1942 and she married Kenneth Darrell Waters on 20 October 1943.

Perhaps the most famous of Enid's characters, *Noddy*, - first appeared in 1949 and from then on *Noddy* books appeared regularly together with many

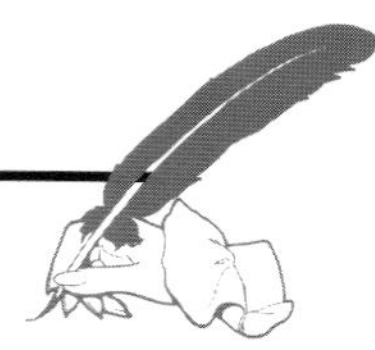

others until 1967. It was in September of that year that her husband, Kenneth, died and Enid herself was very ill. Four more books were published in the following year but she died on 28 November 1968.

In total 606 books written by Enid Blyton were published and in two years, 1951 and 1955, no fewer than 37 appeared. Over 30 were published in each of the years 1949, 1950 and 1952. For many years she edited the *Enid Blyton Magazine* and *Sunny Stories* and contributed a weekly page to *Teachers' World* in addition to writing articles for other publications!

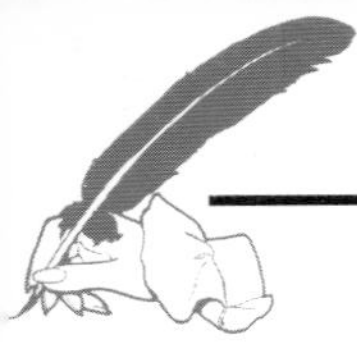

Anne BRADSTREET

Poetess

Anne Bradstreet was born in about 1612 and during her childhood lived at Tattershall Castle, where her father, Thomas Dudley, was steward to the 4th Earl of Lincoln. She moved with her family, in 1619, to Boston when Thomas became manager of the Earl's property in that town. Simon Bradstreet, who was appointed steward in place of Anne's father at Tattershall, married her in 1628.

Anne, with her husband and parents, in 1630 emigrated to America and lived during the first winter in Charlestown, Massachusetts. Anne had suffered from rheumatic fever during her childhood and had also been seriously ill with smallpox. As a result, throughout her life, she suffered from frequent periods of ill health and it was only by her determination and strength of character that she survived the three month voyage to the New World and the privations of her new life.

After several moves Anne and Simon settled in North Andover, Massachusetts in 1644. Her father and husband both became prominent citizens in Massachusetts and Anne was often left alone to look after her eight children. She recorded her experiences and feelings both in verse and prose and it has been said her writings are 'important as the first literary work of any significance to come out of New England'.

Many of her poems record every day events such as her recovery from an illness or the safe return of her husband from one of his lengthy tours round the colony. Her first known poem was entitled *Upon a Fit of Sickness, Anno. 1632* and her last, dated Aug. 31, 1669, was entitled *As Weary Pilgrim*.

Her reputation lies, however, not so much in what she called 'family poems' but in her long epic poems *The Four Seasons, The Four Ages of Man, The Four Elements* and *The Four Humours of Man*. Anne was a great lover of nature and it is interesting to note that in *The Four Seasons* the flowers, the birds and the weather are those of her native Lincolnshire. A stanza from the section on April runs :

This is the month whose fruitful show'rs produces
All set and sown for all delights and uses:
The pear, the plum, and appletree now flourish;
The grass grows long the hungry beast to nourish.
The primrose pale and the azure violet
Among the verdurous grass hath Nature set,
That when the Sun on's love (the earth) doth shine
These might as lace set out his garment fine.
The fearful bird his little house now builds
In trees and walls, in cities, and in fields.
The outside strong, the inside warm and neat,
A natural artificer complete.

Several of her poems were written for her husband and one entitled *In my solitary hours in my dear Husband and his absence* gives a clear indication of her religious convictions and the comfort which this gave to her.

In 1647 her brother-in-law. Rev. John Woodbridge, without her knowledge, took a large selection of Anne's poems

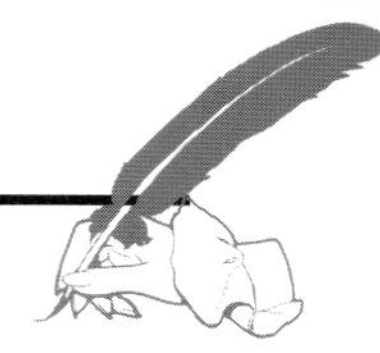

to London and had them published anonymously under the title *The Tenth Muse, lately sprung up in America, by a Gentlewoman in those parts, or Several Poems completed with great variety of wit and learning, full of delight*. Although Anne was annoyed that she had not been consulted beforehand she prepared the copy for a second edition but this was not published until six years after her death.

Anne's *magnum opus* was to have been an epic poem on *The Four Monarchies* based on Sir Walter Raleigh's *History of the World*. She completed the first three *Monarchies* and prefaced the fourth with ten lines which suggest her health was causing problems and 'will force me to a confused brevity.' *The Four Monarchies* are followed by *An Apology* in which she says she

At length resolved, when many years had past,
To prosecute my story to the last;
And for the same, I hours not few did spend,
And weary lines (though lank) I many penned;
But 'fore I could accomplish my desire,
My papers fell a prey to th' raging fire...

The fire which destroyed her house, furnishings, books and manuscripts is recorded in *Some Verses upon the Burning of our House July 10th, 1666*.

A series of *Meditations Divine and Moral* written for her son Simon when he first became a minister in Connecticut, was published along with her poems in 1869 under the title of *The Works of Anne Bradstreet in Prose and Verse*.

Anne died on 16 September 1672 and in a stained-glass window in St. Botolph's Church, Boston, Lincolnshire commemorating four notable women of the town, Anne is shown holding a bird's nest. This was inspired by Anne's poem *In Reference to her Children 23 June 1659* and seems appropriate to conclude this short article about this remarkable lady with the following extracts :

I had eight birds hatched in one nest,
Four cocks there were, and hens the rest.
I nursed them up with pain and care,
Nor cost, nor labour did I spare,
Till at the last they felt their wing,
Mounted the trees and learned to sing...

One to the academy flew
To chat among that learned crew;
Ambition moves still in his breast
That he might chant above the rest,
Striving for more than to do well,
That nightingales he might excel...
***
My other three still with me nest,
Until they're grown, then as the rest,
Or here or there they'll take their flight,
As is ordained, so shall they light...
***
Farewell, my birds, farewell adieu,
I happy am, if well with you.

FURTHER READING
Hensley, Jeannine (Ed.) The Works of Anne Bradstreet (1967)

Frances BROOKE

Authoress

Frances Moore, the eldest daughter of the Revd Thomas Moore and his wife Mary Knowles, was christened on 24 January 1724 at Claypole, Lincolnshire where her father was the curate. Later in the same year Thomas Moore became rector of Carlton Scrope but died in 1725. His widow and children moved to Peterborough to live with Mrs Moore's mother.

Mrs Moore died in 1736 and her children then went to live with their aunt Sarah who had recently married the Revd Roger Stevens, rector of Tydd St Mary. At the age of 24 Frances went to live in London with the intention of becoming a writer. She was very soon accepted into the theatrical and literary world of London of the mid-eighteenth century and became a friend of John Duncombe whose father was a close friend of Samuel Richardson around whom the theatrical and literary circle of the time was centred. By 1756 Frances had become the second wife of the Revd John Brooke vicar of St Augustine's Norwich and incumbent of a number of other Norwich parishes.

Frances' first interest was the theatre and her ambition was to have a play produced at either Covent Garden or Drury Lane. This ambition was not fulfilled until 1781 when her play *The Siege of Sinope* was presented at Covent Garden. Her first successes, however, came in journalism and she edited a weekly publication entitled *Old Maid* from 15 November 1755 to 4 July 1756.

Frances' husband was appointed chaplain with the army in Quebec and on 6 July 1763 she, with her son, John and sister sailed for Canada to join him. Amongst those who called on the evening before her departure to wish her well were Dr Johnson and his friend Mr Boswell which is confirmation of the reputation she had gained for her writing.

In 1769 the first novel to be set in Canada, *The History of Emily Montague*, was published. The novel by Frances comprised 228 letters dated from 10 April 1766 to November 1767 and written by three sets of lovers two of whom are in Canada and the third in England. Clearly the book is based on Frances Brooke's experiences on the voyage to and whilst living in Canada.

Frances Brooke and her husband returned to England in late 1768 and took up residence in London. Frances soon renewed her interest in the London literary scene whilst her husband was occupied with his livings in Norfolk. They were separated for long periods but Frances seems to have been content with her London social life and her writing. A total of fourteen works appeared under her name and she died on 23 January 1789 two days after her hus-

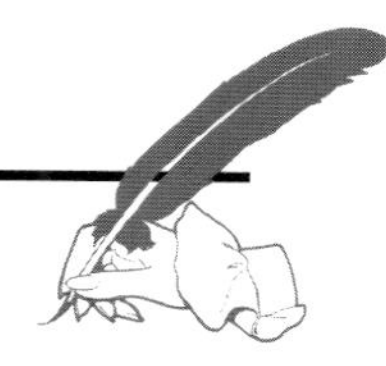

band who is buried in the Chancel of Colney church whilst she is buried in the Chancel of St Denys' Church, Sleaford.

A plaque in the chancel bears the following inscription :

Below lie
the remains of
Mrs Frances Brooke
relict of the Revd John Brooke, D.D.
rector of Colney near Norwich
and daughter of the Rev. Thos. Moore
formerly rector of Carlton Scrope
in this county.
The union of superior literary talents
with goodness of heart, rendered her
works serviceable to the cause of those
virtues of which her life was a shining
example.
She died aged 65, Jan. 23 1789
but two days after her husband
whose remains lie in
Colney chancel.

FURTHER READING

McMullen L *An Odd Attempt in a Woman* 1983

Deborah BULL

Principal Royal Ballet

Although Deborah Bull was actually born in Derby she moved to Lincolnshire in 1970 when her father became vicar of St Clement's Church, Skegness and, later, rector of Ingoldmells. Deborah began dancing at the age of seven and her first ballet classes were with the Janice Sutton School of Dance in Skegness. It was Janice who suggested that Deborah should apply to train with the Royal Ballet School at the age of eleven. After winning the Prix de Lausanne in 1980 she continued her training with Marika Besobrasova in Monte Carlo. Deborah joined The Royal Ballet in September 1981 and rose through the ranks to reach Principal status in 1992.

Deborah dances a wide range of work, including the leading roles in *Swan Lake, The Sleeping Beauty and Don Quixote*. She has received particular praise for her performances of the works of George Balanchine and William Forsythe. In 1995 she danced the leading role in the first British performance of his ballet *Steptext* and she was subsequently nominated in 1996 for an Olivier Award in the 'Outstanding Achievement in Dance' category for her performance. Deborah was named as 1996 Dancer of the Year by the dance critics of both *The Sunday Express* and *The Independent on Sunday* having previously been chosen by the readers of *Dance and Dancers* as one of their Dancers of the Year in both 1991 and 1992.

Television appearances with The Royal Ballet include Ashley Page's pas de deux *Walk and Talk* at the 1997 Farewell Gala, where she also appeared in the finale of *Symphony in C*. On Boxing Day 1997 she appeared on BBC Television in *Steptext* and the Fourth Movement to *Symphony in C*.

In January 1996 Deborah debated at the Oxford Union and she was invited to give the third annual Arts Council lecture in October 1996 by the Royal Society for the Arts. Deborah serves on the Arts Council's Dance Panel, and is involved with several other professional committees.

In addition to her work with The Royal Ballet, she has toured with such notable dancers as Wayne Eagling, Irek Mukhamedov and Tetsuya Kumakawa, and was invited to perform in the first Diamonds of the World Ballet Gala at the Kremlin Palace, Moscow, in April 1996. In 1994 and 1995 she organised, staged and starred in *An Evening of British Ballet* at the Sintra Festival in Portugal.

In January 1998 she was awarded an Honorary Doctorate by the University of Derby 'in recognition of her outstanding achievements as a dancer and her articulate and cogent public advocacy of the place of the arts in society'.

Deborah's interest in nutrition began

as the result of meeting Torje Eike in 1993, when he was working as a physiotherapist with The Royal Ballet. She has developed her interest to such an extent that she now lectures on nutrition to the students of the Royal Ballet School. Her book *The Vitality Plan* was published in January 1998 and her second book, *Dancing Away* is due *for* publication in Autumn 1998.

Deborah has a sister who still lives in Skegness who she visits whenever she can. Although as a child she says that she didn't really appreciate Lincolnshire she now enjoys the calmer environment and slower pace of life. Although Deborah now devotes more time to writing she has no plans for retiring from her dancing.

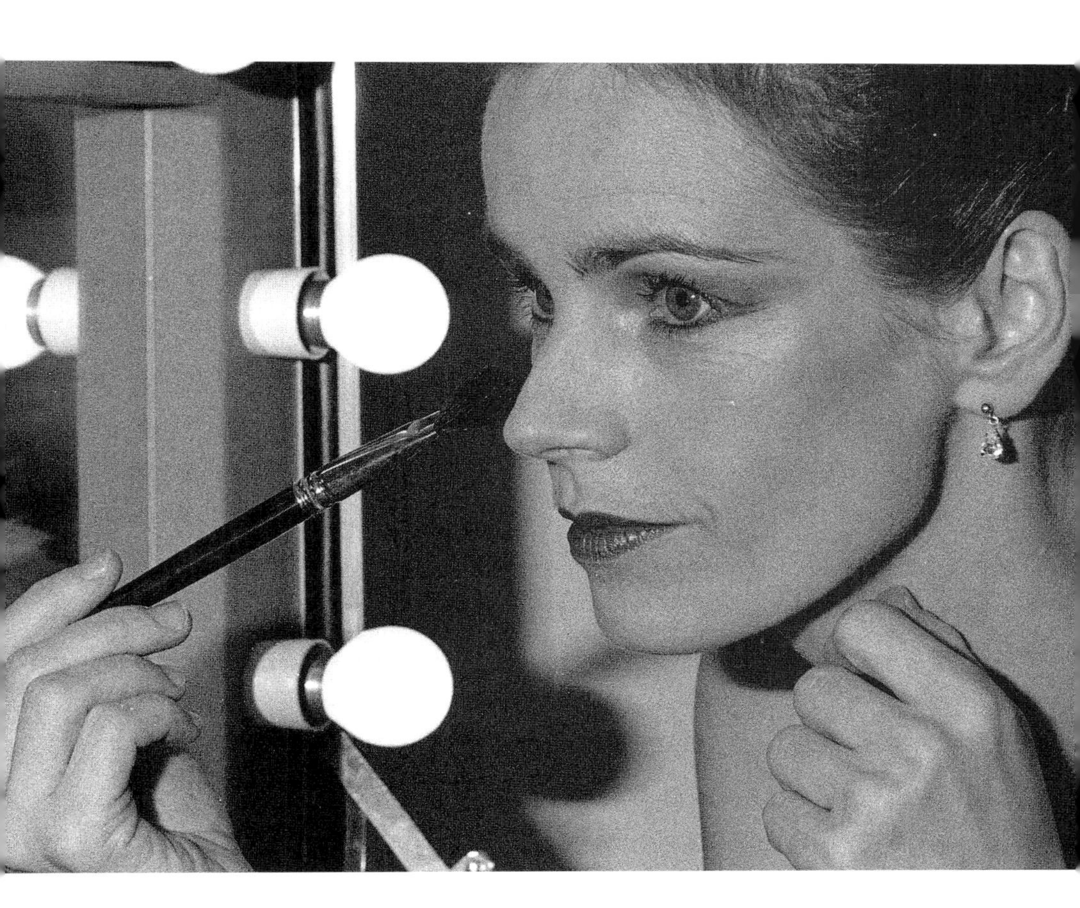

Judy CAMPBELL

Actress

It is not surprising that Judy Campbell went on the stage as both her parents were in the profession, having met as touring actors in the old days of melodrama. Judy's mother, Mary Fulton, was herself from a theatrical family and her father, Jack, had run away from his parents farm in Norfolk, changing his name from Gamble to Campbell. Though very good-looking he couldn't act and so set his sights on management , making Mary promise to be his leading lady if he ever formed his own company. She gave up the opportunity to join Cleethorpes-born impresario George Edwards at the *Gaiety* and she also encouraged Jack to write his own melodramas. Success came with *The Coastguard's Daughter* and he wrote fifteen more. Before he was thirty J. A. Campbell was an established figure and had saved enough money to enable him to lease the *Theatre Royal* in Grantham.

Jack and Mary married and the theatre was their first home. Their son, John, was born there in 1910 and by the time Judy came along six years later they had bought a house and built the *Picture House* in Grantham. Judy remembers spending more of her childhood in the cinema than at home. This wasn't surprising as her mother, who had stopped acting when John was born, poured all her energy into running a cafe in the spacious premises over the cinema. There was a large balcony over-looking St. Peter's Hill and the statue of Sir Isaac Newton and soon Mary was catering for weddings as well as lunches and teas. Judy loved to help decorate cakes and be pushed up and down in the food lift.

Judy's mother also made the foyer of the cinema a welcoming place with flowers in summer and in winter an enormous Christmas tree from the Belvoir Castle estate. The Duke of Rutland was a regular cinema goer as were the poor children who got in for a penny on Saturdays and were given a Christmas party with presents from the tree.

In the First World War both theatre and cinema were used for war charities and troops had free entry. Judy's father had been turned down for military service and he made up for it by taking concert parties on Sundays to camps and hospitals. For this he was awarded the OBE.

As a child Judy was allowed to 'help' Winnie in the box-office counting the chocolate bars and eating the broken ones! She actually made her first appearance in the cinema at the age of ten singing *Peter Pan I love you* before the film.

Judy's education started at the Kesteven and Grantham Girls' School and continued at boarding school in Sussex. Her first grown-up stage appearance was back in Grantham at her father's theatre in weekly rep. Several years in rep followed, notably in Brighton and Cambridge. By the outbreak of war in 1939 she had graduated to being leading lady at the prestigious Liverpool Playhouse. Judy's London debut came in the Spring of 1940 with the revue *New Faces* in which she was the first to sing *A Nightingale Sang in*

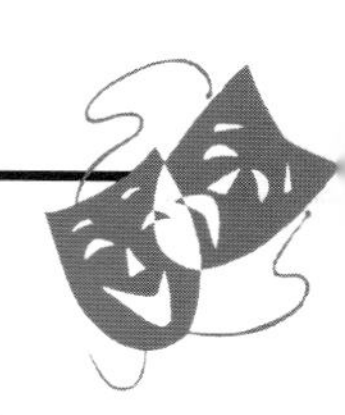

Berkley Square. Without any training in song or dance she somehow made it magic. The air raids were starting and 'She lifted the fear out of our hearts' wrote the distinguished critic, Harold Hobson. It is still remembered and recently Judy performed it at Drury Lane and was asked to repeat it for the *Esther Rantzen Show* on Television.

New Faces and *The Nightingale* really triggered off Judy's success. Noel Coward chose her for his leading lady in *Present Laughter* and *This Happy Breed*. She toured with him in *Blithe Spirit* and accompanied him to troop concerts.

Subsequent successes have included *Relative Values* - also by Noel Coward - *The Reluctant Debutante*, Bernard Shaw's *Heartbreak House* and *You Never can Tell* with Sir Ralph Richardson. Sandy Wilson's *Valmouth* and *The Sleeping Prince* with Omar Sharif. Judy has made over thirty television appearances including the series *Nanny, The House of Elliott, Bergerac* and *Casualty*.

Judy's most recent visit to Grantham accompanied by her children, Andrew and Jane, was on 16 March 1996 when she unveiled a plaque on the site of the former Picture House commemorating 100 years of cinema. There were many tributes to the Campbell family including one from Baroness Thatcher who, as Margaret Roberts, had delivered groceries on her bicycle to the Campbell home when in her early 'teens'. Judy's mother had be-friended her and it was because of this that Mr Roberts was persuaded to let his young daughter go to the cinema.

Judy married Lt Commander David Birkin, DSC, in 1943 and two of their three children followed her professionally. Her son, Andrew, is a writer and director and her daughter Jane's career is in films, theatre and recording mainly in France where she has been made *Chevalier des Arts et Lettres*. Judy also has nine grandchildren three of whom are showing signs of following in their grandmother's footsteps.

'CLARIBEL'
Song Writer

'Claribel' was the pen-name of Mrs. Charles Cary Barnard the wife of the Rector of Kirmington. Between 1859 and 1869 she became one of the most popular Victorian song and ballad writers of her day.

Charlotte Alington was born at Louth on 23 December 1830. She was the only daughter of Henry Alington Pye who was a solicitor in Louth and his wife Charlotte Mary Yerburgh of Frampton. Nothing is known of her education but by the age of nine she had produced her first known poem which recorded the custom of distributing three yards of cloth to 500 poor women on 21 December each year. The poem ran to no less than 20 verses!

On the 26 March 1842 at the age of eleven years Charlotte started to attend as a day pupil the newly opened Ladies' Academy run by Miss Elizabeth Leak at 'The Sycamores'. Whilst Charlotte was still a pupil four years later the school moved to Panton Hall.

On 8 July 1847 Charlotte laid the foundation stone of Louth Railway Station with a silver trowel inscribed 'The first stone was laid by Miss Pye, daughter of Henry Pye, Esq., of Louth'. Two months later Charlotte and her father were given places of honour in one of the two carriages when the first train ran over the newly laid railway line.

On 29 December 1847 Charlotte's mother died after a long illness and was buried in Swinhope Church. At the age of eighteen Charlotte 'came-out' and it was decided that this important event in her life was to be in January 1849 and the occasion the South Wold Hunt Ball which was held in the Mansion House, Louth. Her particular friends were the Holloway family who had taken up residence at Gunby Hall and it was on a visit here that Charlotte met Jean Ingelow who presented her with a copy of her recently published book of poems called *A Rhyming Chronicle*.

Charlotte had become particularly friendly with John Holloway who was a barrister at the Middle Temple and they corresponded regularly. Her father was concerned that Holloway was not a suitable prospective husband for his daughter and preferred Charles Barnard the eldest son of the Rector of Bigby who had graduated in 1850 with a B. A. at Exeter College, Oxford. However, Charlotte, against her father's wishes, became engaged to John Holloway. She was persuaded to break off the engagement and on 18 May 1854 she married Charles Barnard at St George's Hanover Square, London and two days later her father married Lady Albina Francis Hobart at Sidmouth.

Charlotte and her husband lived at 'The Firs' in Westgate, Louth although he was in fact rector of St Olave, Ruckland and St Peter, Farforth with Maidenwell which were about six miles from Louth. Charlotte was presented at Court on 29 May 1856 and in 1857 the Barnards decided to leave Louth and live in London. Whilst their house and furniture was being sold they decided to take a holiday in Germany where Charlotte

was able to give full reign to her sketching and wrote a ballad called 'The Lily of St Goar' which she later set to music. Towards the end of the year the Barnards took up residence at 6 Ecclestone Square in Pimlico. which was at that time a fashionable area in which to live. Charlotte was able to renew her friendship with the Ingelow family. Jean Ingelow was now editing the *Youths Magazine* and was a member of a literary Society called The Portfolio to which she introduced Charlotte. In 1859 a song written by Charlotte based on The Brook by Tennyson was published by Mr Emery of Oxford Street and as was usual at this time she used a pseudonym. Thus was born 'Claribel' by which Charlotte became so well known. In March of the same year she submitted her next song, 'Janet's Choice' to the firm of Addison, Hollier and Lucas who rejected it but her original publisher accepted it. Addison, Hollier and Lucas seem to have soon regretted their earlier decision and before the end of the year they published another of 'Claribel's' songs 'There's a Silver Lining to every Cloud'.

On 4 January 1860 Charlotte received a letter from the noted singer Miss Charlotte Dolby suggesting that she should study under a good music master and requesting a copy of 'Janet's Choice'. Charlotte did, in fact, have lessons in piano and composition from Mr W. H. Holmes a successful concert pianist and song writer.

Charles Barnard was offered the living of Brocklesby with Kirmington by the Earl of Yarborough and he decided to accept. They moved back to Lincolnshire and took up residence in Kirmington Rectory in January 1864. Charlotte continued with her song writing and 'Claribel' was advertised as the most popular composer of the day. Amongst the fifteen songs published in 1864 two were musical settings of poems by Lincolnshire writer Jean Ingelow. She appears to have had published 96 songs, a book of verse and short essays called *Fireside Thoughts and Ballads* and *A Book of Thoughts, Verse and Songs* was printed for private circulation in 1877.

In 1868 Charlotte's father, Henry Pye, was declared bankrupt and he fled to the continent with his second wife and settled in Belgium where Charlotte and her husband joined him. In January 1869 the Barnards returned to England for a short holiday but Charlotte was taken seriously ill and died after a short illness.

FURTHER READING

Smith, P. and Godsmark, M. *The Story of Claribel (Charlotte Alington Barnard)* (Lincoln, 1965)

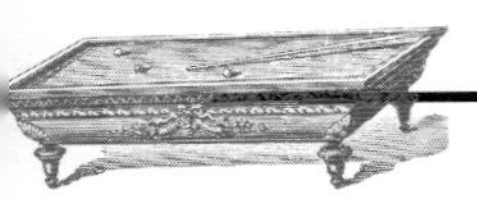

Karen CORR

Snooker Champion

Karen Corr was actually born in Northern Ireland in 1969 but at the age thirteen moved with her family to Bourne. After leaving the Robert Manning School in Bourne in 1985 Karen worked for her father as a dental receptionist until he retired five years later.

Karen began playing snooker and billiards at the age of fourteen and her early progress was guided by Peterborough based Mark Wildman. Mark is a former World Billiards Champion who felt that one of her strongest assets is her enthusiasm to continue learning about the game even after achieving top honours.

Before Karen decided to turn professional in 1990 she had won a number of league and World Ladies Billiards and Snooker Association titles. In 1989 she was top lady player in the professional qualifying competitions and reached the semi-finals of the Ladies World Championships. In the same year she was champion in the Ladies World Speed Challenge and the Sunday Times Sportswoman of the year.

These successes were the foundation of her professional career and she has taken part in the Ladies' World Championships eight times; reaching the semi-finals three times, was runner-up once and champion four times. In 1991 Karen reached the semi-final of the World Mixed Doubles with partner Jimmy White and in the Ladies United Kingdom Championships she reached the semi-final in 1989, was runner up in 1995 and champion in 1993, 1994 and 1997.

In 1993 Karen played in a 28 hour continuous snooker marathon which raised £1850 for the charity Telethon.

Karen has now travelled world-wide to take part in Championships and Exhibitions. One of her most strenuous tours was in 1997 when she played 25 exhibitions in 30 days during a tour of Australia and New Zealand.

When, in 1996, Terry Griffiths established the World Professional Billiards and Snooker Association Coaching Scheme Karen was selected and is the only woman member.

Karen has appeared on Jim Davidson's television shows *Big Break* (six times) and *Generation Game* with further appearances scheduled for both programmes in the near future. She has also been a commentator on Sky and Australian Television. Live on BBC television Karen and Lord Archer in March 1998 drew the contestants for the first round of the World Snooker Championships.

In appreciation of her work as an ambassador for her home town and the 'forgotten county' Karen was awarded the freedom of Bourne in 1991.

Karen has received much encouragement from her family and she is sponsored by Bourne Services Group. One of her future ambitions is to become Snooker Champion at the Olympics in 2004. Karen's dedication and enthusiasm coupled with her personality suggests that she is very likely to achieve this ambition and to continue her successes world wide.

Barbara DICKSON

Actress, Singer

Barbara Dickson first came to Lincolnshire during the 1970s when she lived at Navenby for a short period. She came to love the open spaces of the county and so, when her career was established, Barbara and her husband decided to leave London and, in 1992, they returned to the 'forgotten county'. They live with their three young sons near Louth.

Barbara taught herself to play the guitar and became hooked on folk music as a teenager. During the day she worked in the civil service but in the evening she performed in folk clubs around her home town, Dunfermline. Her big break came with Willy Russell's musical '*John, Paul, George, Ringo... and Bert*' in 1974. This was followed by number of highly popular singles including '*Answer Me*', '*The Caravan Song*', '*Another Suitcase in Another Hall*', and '*January, February*'. She also recorded an album '*All for Song*' which sold over 500,000 copies in Britain alone.

In 1975 Barbara made her first television appearance on '*The Two Ronnies*' and in 1983 she took the part of Mrs Johnstone in Willy Russell's musical '*Blood Brothers*'. This was staged in Liverpool and Barbara's performance earned her the prestigious Olivier Award. It was here that she met her husband, Oliver Cookson, who was a stage manager at the Liverpool Playhouse.

In 1984 she released two further albums '*Heartbeats*' and the '*Barbara Dickson Songbook*'. In the same year she was the guest star in the recording of a new musical, '*Chess*'. In 1985, with Elaine Paige, she scored a hit with one of the songs from the show, '*I know him so well*'. Other albums quickly followed including '*Gold*' The '*Right Moment*', '*Coming Alive Again*' and '*Parcel of Rogues*'.

She played the part of a wealthy ex-pop star in the television series '*Taggart*' and, in 1995, she took part in the first series on TV of '*Band of Gold*' as well as singing the theme tune, '*Love Hurts*', which was released as a single. A second series of '*Band of Gold*' followed. Barbara released another album '*The Dark End of the Street*' in November 1995 and she also appeared in a BBC film for TV called '*The Missing Postman*' which was screened at Easter 1997. Later that year Barbara's career took her to Australia where she played the lead role of Florence in the musical '*Chess*'. In the Autumn of 1997 Barbara finally had time to try a short run of a project which had been on ice for some two years. A theatre production titled '*The 7 Ages of Woman*' which was devised and directed by Chris Bond. The show opened at the Liverpool Playhouse on 13 October 1997 to enormous critical acclaim and commercial success. The show will now be taken on a nation-wide tour in the spring and summer of 1998 prior to transferring to London's West End.

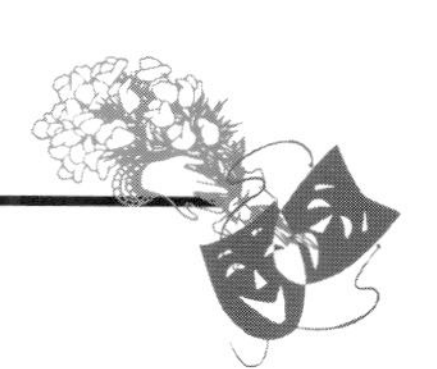

Barbara leads an extremely busy life touring throughout the country but she looks forward to returning to her Lincolnshire home whenever she can.

As well as being a wife and mother she is a keen environmentalist and collector of antiques.

Violet Penelope DICKSON

Botanist

Violet Penelope Lucas-Calcraft was born on 3 September 1896 at Gautby where her father was a land agent to the Vyner family. As a child she collected butterflies and birds eggs. Another recreation was trapping and skinning moles. Violet was educated at Miss Lunn's High School, Woodhall Spa, and at Les Charmettes at Vevey in Switzerland.

In 1915 Violet started work at Smith's Bank in Lincoln. Three years later she was posted to Cox's Bank in Marseilles, and it was here that she met her future husband Captain Dickson who was then serving in the Indian Army.

In 1919 the couple were married in Bombay and Violet's married life began in Mesopotamia. She soon became as enthusiastic as her husband for the Near East, and especially for the Arabs of the desert. Her two children, who were given Arab names - Saud for the son, Zahra for the daughter - were brought up to think of boiled locusts as a special treat!

In 1929 Captain Dickson was appointed political agent in Kuwait which was then a small town with the entire European community consisting of eleven people. Although on arrival they were treated with great ceremonial, their house was a rat infested dilapidated mud building which they had to repair themselves.

Such was the trust which Sheikh Ahmed, Emir of Kuwait, placed in the Dicksons' judgement that one evening over dinner he asked for Violet's help in finding a suitable wife.

Violet made frequent ventures into the desert, both to visit her Bedouin friends, in particular to attend tribal weddings, and in pursuit of new botanical and entomological specimens. She sent dried flowers back to Kew and the Natural History Museum supplied nets, killing bottles and other equipment to assist her quest for desert insects, especially grasshoppers. A plant - *Horwoodia dicksoniae* - and a beetle - *Julodius speculifer dicksoni* were named after her. In 1955 she published *The Wild Flowers of Kuwait and Bahrain*, which carried her own illustrations.

Violet's knowledge of Kuwait, and in particular her unparalleled grasp of the feuds and rivalries festering among the kingdom's 600-strong royal family, made her an indispensable resource for incoming ambassadors and visiting notables.

Attempts were made after her husband's death in 1959 to persuade her to move into a more comfortable and modern abode and it was rumoured that the current ruler Sheikh Jaber Al Ahmad Al Sabah had offered the hospitality of his palace. But Violet preferred to remain in the small seaside house were she and her husband had first moved in 1929.

Her 80th birthday party, held in a tent in the embassy compound in the summer of 1976 was a major event in the life of the British community; and the heavens laid on an almighty thunderstorm for the occasion.

Violet's autobiography Forty Years in Kuwait, was published in 1971. Her services to Anglo-Kuwaiti relations were recognised by her appointment MBE in 1942, as CBE in 1964 and as DBE in 1976.

Dame Violet Dickson died in 1991.

Annie DIXON

Miniature Painter

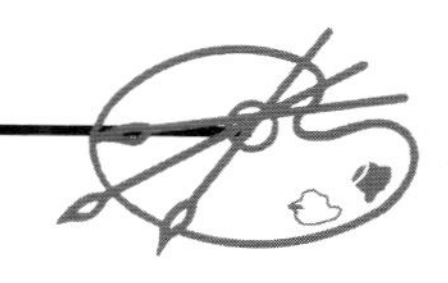

Annie Dixon was born in Horncastle on 12 March 1817. Nothing is known about her early life but she is said to have been a pupil of Sir W. C. Ross. In about 1840 she went to London and travelled to the homes of her clients in order to paint their portraits in miniature. Amongst her patrons were the Royal family and many of the aristocracy.

In 1862 she painted all the Strathmore family and she is said to have painted a ring on the finger of the Dowager Marchioness of Cambridge, then a child, to keep her quiet whilst being painted! Miss Dixon was a very prolific painter and she is said to have produced over 1000 miniatures. Her sitters included Queen Alexandra, as Princess of Wales, and Louisa, Marchioness of Waterford.

Her most successful works were miniatures of children. A miniature of Horace Charles West as a child signed and dated 1861 was given by Queen Victoria to Lady Caroline Barrington, a woman of the Bedchamber, whose grandson was the sitter.

Annie Dixon died in 1901 and examples of her work are in the Victoria and Albert Museum.

FURTHER READING

Foskett, D. *Miniature Dictionary and Guide* (1987)

Jane EAGLEN

Opera Singer

Jane Eaglen was brought up in 'down hill' Lincoln and attended St Peter at Gowt's Infant and Junior Schools, which have long since been demolished. Jane says that she did manage to rescue a small piece of brick from the building which she still has.

Jane first showed an interest in music by playing on a neighbour's piano, and began to sing along with Gilbert and Sullivan scores when aged four or five. At the age of five she began piano lessons with Miss Lamming and studied with her for a few years before going to John Thursby and Geoffrey Greed.

The same neighbour took Jane to Sunday School at the Central Methodist Church in Lincoln from the age of three and only two weeks after her first visit she made her first public performance by reciting *The Daisy* at the Sunday School Anniversary.

She continued to perform at Church and the organist, Roy Newport, was the first person to ask her to sing solo. Jane joined the choir and often sang during the services. She also took part in local music festivals and concerts.

At the age of eleven Jane continued her education at the South Park High School for Girls and sang her first opera there at the age of thirteen. Jane's role was Phoebe Crome in Phyllis Tate's *Twice in a Blue Moon*.

Piano continued to be Jane's main musical interest, but she did learn the violin for a while. At the age of seventeen, after she had completed her piano exams, Geoffrey Greed suggested that Jane took singing lessons. She took his advice and travelled to Grantham every Saturday for over a year to study with Anne Abbott.

It was Anne Abbott who encouraged Jane to take up singing as a career and apply for music college as a singer and not as a pianist. She applied for entry to the Royal Northern College of Music where she studied with Joseph Ward, OBE with whom she continues to work.

Jane won several awards at the College including the Peter Moores Foundation Scholarship, Countess of Munster award and Carl Rosa Trust Award. Immediately on leaving college she auditioned for the English National Opera and was offered a principal contract. Her first role was as Lady Ella in Gilbert and Sullivan's operetta *Patience*.

Memorable performances by Jane include Brunnhilde in Wagner's *Ring Cycle;* Donna Anna in *Don Giovanni;* Amelia in *Ballo in Maschera;* Tosca and Santuzza in *Cavalleria Rusticana* and the title role in *Turandot*. Her appearances as *Norma* have won her particular acclaim with *Sunday Times* predicting that she would be the *Norma* of the 1990's.

Jane has now sung world wide and her career keeps her very busy but she likes to return to visit her family in Lincoln whenever she can. She has sung in all of the major venues of the

world including the Metropolitan Opera, New York; La Scala, Milan; the State Opera, Vienna; the Bastille (Paris Opera); the State Opera, Berlin; Teatro Colon, Buenos Aires; Carnegie Hall, New York; Tivoli Festival, Copenhagen; Hollywood Bowl and London's South Bank.

Jane says she still looks forward to singing in Lincoln Cathedral and is very proud of her origins. She is an enthusiastic ambassador for Lincoln and this was recognised recently when she received the Lincoln Civic Award. Jane also maintains her links with the City as Patron of the Lincoln Orpheus Male Voice Choir. Her first public performance was with that Choir in Lincoln Cathedral and she makes regular guest appearances which have helped to raise many thousands of pounds for local charities - in particular for the St Barnabas Trust.

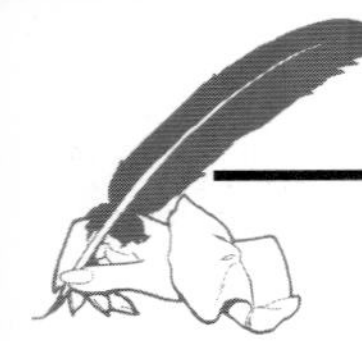

George ELIOT

(Marian Evans) Author

Lincolnshire's connection with Marian Evans, who is better known under the alias George Eliot, is in the location which she used for *The Mill on the Floss*. It is widely believed that Marian Evans whilst staying in Gainsborough in late 1858 or early 1859 decided that the town should be the fictional St Oggs, with the River Trent being the River Floss.

Marian Evans was born in Nuneaton on 22 November 1819 and was the daughter of Robert Evans a Warwickshire land agent. She was sent to boarding school at Attleborough at the age of five and at the age of eight to another boarding school in Nuneaton and finally, in 1832, to yet another boarding school in Coventry. She left to return home in 1835 taking up the running of her father's household in the following year when her mother died. Her father employed various tutors to teach her German, Italian and music.

In 1841 the family moved to Coventry and after the death of her father in 1849 Marian went to Geneva for a short time returning in 1850 to live in London. She began to write under the name of George Eliot for the *Westminster Review* and became assistant editor in 1851. She travelled widely in the company of G. H. Lewes and on returning to live in Richmond began to write a number of popular books. The first of these *Adam Bede* was published in 1859, *The Mill on the Floss* appeared in 1860, to be followed by *Silas Marner* (1861), *Romulas* (1863) and *Felix Holt* (1866).

On 6 May 1880 Marian Evans married John Cross but she died on 22 December in the same year.

Violet Van der ELST

Campaigner

This fascinating lady bought Harlaxton Manor in 1937 but she was actually born Violet Anne Dodge in a suburb of London on 4 January 1882. She was the daughter of John and Louise Dodge who lived in Bedfont Lane, Feltham Surrey. Violet spent much of her childhood with her older sister Mabel who at the age of 12 had become a housemaid for Canon and Mrs Limpus. After the death of his wife the Canon married Mabel who was some forty years his junior. It was from Canon Limpus that Violet gained her love of music and composing.

Violet started work as a scullery maid but soon ran away and turned to a career on the stage. At the age of seventeen she married Arthur Nathan an engineer. He died in 1927 and four months later Violet married Jean Julien Romain Van der Elst a Belgian who worked for her late husband.

A very successful business was started by Violet in the kitchen of her house in Belsize Park, London manufacturing face creams, ointment, beauty lotions, soap and 'Shavex'. She was passionately opposed to capital punishment and in 1935 launched a vigorous campaign to which she was to devote her life and fortune for over a quarter of a century. Hardly ever during that time was her familiar figure absent from the scene when, supported by a regiment of sandwichmen on the ground and her silver planes trailing black flags overhead to the accompaniment of her brass band playing the Dead March In Saul and hymns, she protested against a hanging about to take place within some prison's walls.

Soon after the death sentence had been passed she would tour the town in her Rolls Royce exhorting the public through a loudspeaker to sign a petition calling for a reprieve. On her behalf, a month after the opening of her campaign, Clement Attlee, MP presented to Parliament a petition with more than 100,000 signatures which she had obtained. There is no doubt that Mrs. Van der Elst's sensational methods though frowned upon by some did have the merit of focusing public attention on an unpopular subject, and that she can be regarded as the person who did more than anyone else to secure the abolition of capital punishment in Britain. In efforts to further her campaign Mrs. Van der Elst started her own newspaper and stood unsuccessfully three times for Parliament.

In October 1937 Mrs Van der Elst bought Harlaxton Manor near Grantham and promptly renamed it Grantham Castle. She filled it with antique furniture some of which was obtained from Buckingham Palace, Rufford Abbey, Clumber Park and even with some carpets from the Winter Palace in St Petersburg. She purchased a chandelier originally intended for the Royal Bank in Madrid which she claimed to be the

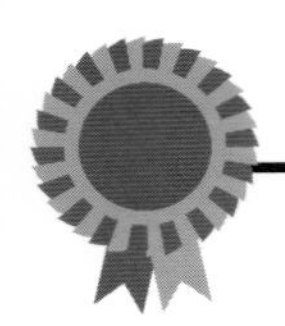

largest in the world. To give the castle a medieval air some thirty suits of armour together with swords, battle axes, crossbows, pikes, halberds and maces were prominently displayed. The Castle was opened to the public and admission was free for old age pensioners and the blind.

Although the people of Harlaxton regarded her, not surprisingly, as very eccentric she displayed great kindness to anyone in trouble. In 1948 she sold Harlaxton to the Jesuits and made her headquarters in Richmond Park, Surrey. Her long campaign for the abolition of capital punishment made great inroads on her wealth. The execution of Ruth Ellis in 1955 appears to have triggered off public awareness for her campaign and in the following year the Homicide Act became law. This abolished capital punishment for most offences and in 1965 the Murder (Abolition of Death Penalty) Act finally abolished capital punishment in Great Britain.

Violet van der Elst died on 30 April 1966 in a state of near penury, virtually friendless and ignored by the press. A sad end for such a colourful and dedicated personality.

FURTHER READING

Gattey, C. N. The Incredible Mrs Van der Elst (1972)

Brenda FISHER

Swimming Champion

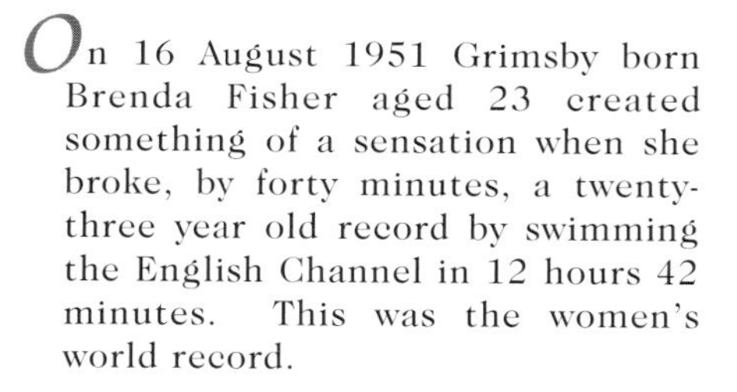

On 16 August 1951 Grimsby born Brenda Fisher aged 23 created something of a sensation when she broke, by forty minutes, a twenty-three year old record by swimming the English Channel in 12 hours 42 minutes. This was the women's world record.

This feat was only achieved by hard training and dedication. Brenda remembers the manager of Cleethorpes bathing pool with gratitude. He would open up the pool for her at five o'clock in the morning so that she could train before the public were admitted.

Brenda went back to the pool at lunchtime and again in the evening! At weekends she practiced endurance swimming in Alexandra Dock for up to eight hours at a time. During this strenuous training Brenda was also going out with Pat Johnston, who at one time was a player with Grimsby Town football team. They married in 1954 but sadly Pat died in 1971.

Brenda became a celebrity overnight. She was voted Sportswomen of the Year, appeared many times on television and radio shows, including the Ed Sullivan Show in America and even appeared on the Royal Variety Command Performance. Brenda was particularly pleased that her status as a celebrity enabled her to travel world wide and meet many well known people.

Although swimming the Channel was the most exciting event of her swimming career, the 32 mile swim across Lake Ontario in Canada was the toughest. This event took 18 hours 52 minutes and the water was extremely cold. There was one compensation; the water was fresh and drinkable!

Before retiring in 1959 Brenda took part in and won the women's Channel race again and competed in races all over the world including the Capri to Naples and the River Nile swims.

Brenda has continued to take an interest in swimming and trains youngsters in speed swimming.

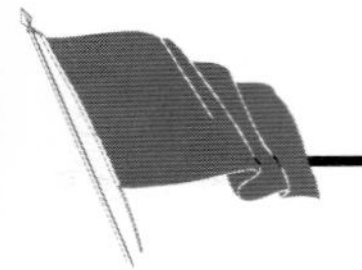

Rosita FORBES

Explorer and Authoress

Rosita Forbes, the daughter of H. J. Torr, of Morton Hall, Lincolnshire was born in 1893 and began to travel while still in her teens. When she was quite young she married Colonel Robert Forbes with whom she visited India, Australia and Africa. The first World War came and, as a challenge, she chose to drive an Ambulance for the *Societe de Secours aux blesses militaires*, a service for which she received two war medals.

In 1917 she divorced her husband and in the following year she set forth with a woman friend upon a lonely journey across the Pacific to the Dutch East Indies and on through the Far East. Her experiences there formed the subject of her first book *Unconducted Wanderers* which was published in 1919 and attracted considerable interest.

In 1920 she travelled, first to North Africa and Arabia and then on a more hazardous venture to Kufara in Libya, a place which no European had attempted to reach since 1879. She had the good fortune to make friends with the all-important Sheikh, Sidi Idriss, and to obtain his help in penetrating the interior of his country. Eventually she reached Taj, where she lived the life of a veiled Arab woman; but she kept a camera concealed under her voluminous cloak.

Rosita Forbes well earned her place as one of the greatest of women explorers. In addition to adding to the knowledge of the geographers, she had obtained much useful information in regard to the Senussi and their outlook. In London, therefore, she was the heroine of the hour. King George V sent for her to hear her story at first hand; learned bodies invited her to deliver lectures, and she received a "national recognition" in the form of a book of signatures of representative people with the Prince of Wales at their head. In addition the Royal Antwerp Geographical Society gave her a Gold Medal. In a series of articles published in *The Times* in March, 1921 she narrated her story in broad outline and later gave fuller information in her book, *Secret of the Sahara Kufara* which was published in 1922. Her novel. *The Jewel in the Lotus* was also published in that year.

In 1921 Rosita Forbes married Colonel Arthur T. McGrath, DSO who was on the General Staff at the War Office. but the following year she was off on another expedition to Asia continuing to Morocco.

Few women can have travelled so widely, seen so much, or produced a survey of the globe comparable with that comprised in her long series of books. She was a keen observer, and a forceful and interesting writer. Vital, indefatigable, and immensely courageous, she was not only one of the leading women explorers of her own time, but one of its most pic-

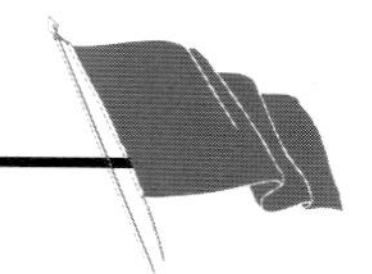

turesque and entertaining personalities.

From Red Sea to Blue Nile published in 1925 recorded a journey of over a thousand miles by horse or mule. *Conflict* which appeared in 1931 recorded Rosita Forbes' experiences in Persia and on her way there through Palestine and Iraq. In 1933 *Eight Republics in Search of a Future* was about evolution and revolution in South America. *Forbidden Road, Kabul to Samarkand* published in 1937, opened up yet another field of exploration. In addition to such travelogues she wrote *These are Real People* (1937) and *These Men I Knew* (1940) in which she described some of those she had met..

There was scarcely a corner of the earth which she had not seen and studied, and *India of the Princes* (1939) was as vivid as her many other works. She eventually made her home in the Bahamas and a new series of books appeared. *A Unicorn in the Bahamas* was published in 1939 and *The Prodigious Caribbean* followed in 1940. In *Gypsy in the Sun* which appeared in 1944 she wrote about the people of the Bahamas. After the Second World War Rosita Forbes wrote three volumes of her autobiography, and a biography of Sir Henry Morgan, the pirate. She was a fellow of the Royal Geographical Society and an Honorary member of several foreign ones.

Her second husband died in 1962 and Rosita Forbes, traveller, lecturer and author died at her home at Warwick, Bermuda in July 1967.

Joan GIBBONS

Botanist

When Joan Gibbons died on 2 December 1988 Lincolnshire lost a lady who had become the County's leading botanist. The Lincolnshire Trust for Nature Conservation lost one of its founder Council members, the Botanical Society of the British Isles and the Wild Flower Society one of their most dedicated and most hardworking recorders. Joan Gibbons was born in Essex but when she was five she moved with her family to Holton-le-Moor. At eleven she attended with her father her first Lincolnshire Naturalists Union meeting. She was encouraged by her mother and her two sisters, Mary and Dora, to record all the plants at Holton-le-Moor and since then kept the botanical lists for which she became famous.

She became a member of the Union in 1920, Botanical Secretary from 1936 until 1985 and President in 1939. She was also President in 1974 when her *Flora of Lincolnshire* was published - the climax of her lifetime's work, the first county flora to be written by a woman. She valued greatly her second term of office - again the first lady to have this well deserved honour. The Supplement published ten years later reflected her continued involvement in recording.

In 1923 following the example of her eldest sister Mary, she joined the Wild Flower Society and was later the recorder for the County. She also joined the BSBI in 1946 and almost immediately was appointed Recorder for the two Lincolnshire Vice-Counties - a duty she wholeheartedly undertook resulting in a huge benefit for the Lincolnshire records published in the *Atlas of British Flora* in 1960. She faced the formidable task in the vast Lincolnshire County of recording in ninety 10km squares with very little support and it is most satisfactory to record here that the Lincolnshire squares are some of the best covered in the country. Helped by her friends Brenda and Ieaver Howitt and John Chandler, former Union President recording in Lincolnshire flourished. In 1969 she was elected a Fellow of the Linnaean Society.

During the war Joan Gibbons helped the then Lindsey and Holland Rural Community Council with the collection of medicinal herbs and started a fund dedicated to the publication of a future Flora. She also spent much time researching the lives of past Lincolnshire botanists with help from her brother George Dixon - a classical scholar.

In 1972 on the death of her brother, Miss Gibbons and her two sisters moved to Glentworth. Here

her interest in her own family history and the histories of the Glentworth families developed. She was a prominent member of the Society for Lincolnshire History and Archaeology.

SOURCE
Adapted, with permission, from an obituary by Irene Weston in *Transactions of the Lincolnshire Naturalists Union* Vol. 22 No. 2 1989 pp126-127.

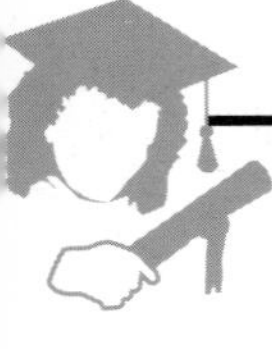

Diane GREEN

University Vice-Chancellor

When Professor Diana Green was installed as vice-chancellor of Sheffield Hallam University in October, 1998 she became one of only six women to hold such high office at a British University.

Diana Margaret Harris was born in Lincoln in 1943 where her father was a Local Government Officer. Her mother and elder sister still live in Lincoln. Diana attended the then South Park High School for Girls before going up to the University of Reading in 1961. She read for a BA Honours degree in French but left before graduating to work in industry. In 1966 she entered the Civil Service and worked for the Land Commission in Reading and at the Civil Service College at Sunningdale.

Diana took leave from 1970 until 1976 to study on a full-time basis for a degree in Economics and then for a PhD. She also assisted her husband in the establishment and running of a small retail company. Although it had been her intention to return to the Civil Service, when Diana was offered a lectureship at the City of London Polytechnic in 1976 together with a part time consultancy with the Department of Trade and Industry this seemed a much more attractive career prospect. In 1982, she was appointed Principal Lecturer in Political Economy and Acting Head of the Department of Politics and Government.

In 1984 Diana moved to Birmingham Polytechnic as Head of the Department of Government and Economics. She was Pro-Vice Chancellor at Birmingham Polytechnic (since 1992 University of Central England) from 1987 until August 1992 with responsibility for strategic planning and quality assurance and from September 1992 Pro-Vice Chancellor with responsibility for planning and resources. The holder of this post has the responsibility for managing an annual budget of some £78 million.

Diana Green took over the management of Hallam University at a time when universities face fundamental changes which include the introduction of tuition fees for students. She says "...the introduction of tuition fees for full-time students will mean universities need to be much more responsive to the needs of people who are essentially their customers".

During an extremely busy career Diana Green initially established an academic reputation for her research and publications on economic and industrial change and has provided consultancy services in this field to the United Kingdom Department of Trade and Industry. More recently she has established an international reputation for her work on quality management in Higher Education. For several years Diana wrote a regular column for the *Times Higher Educational Supplement* and still makes an occasional contribution. She is clearly someone who recognises the problem of maintaining student satisfaction at a time when

they face the prospect of graduating while heavily in debt, coupled with no certainty of being able to follow a career in their chosen subject. Diana comments that "..it has never occurred to me that women could not succeed in senior posts". She goes on to say that "There is very much a glass ceiling in academia which women have to break through and that's partly to do with the fact that the career structure makes it difficult to get back in after having children."

Diana Green has served and is serving on many bodies concerned with Higher Education and was, until recently, a Director of the Alexandra National Health Service Healthcare Trust. From 1992 until 1994 she was a director of the Black Country Development Corporation. In 1990 Diana was elected to Fellowship of the Royal Society of Arts.

Surprisingly, such a very busy lady does have some spare time! Perhaps not so surprising, for someone coming from "Bomber County", is that her way of relaxing and escaping from the stresses of top management is flying. Diana has recently been awarded her pilot's licence.

Agnes Genevieve Grey

Hotel Owner

The film and musical *South Pacific* is based on the book *Tales from the South Pacific* by James Michener. Michener spent much of his time at Aggie Grey's hotel in Samoa and the biography of Aggie by Nelson Eustis, states that her paternal ancestors came from Lincolnshire.

In fact, Aggie's grandfather, James Butler Swann, was born on 13 December 1834 at Carlton le Moorland and became a prosperous chemist and druggist. He married Mary White of Stamford on 22 June 1856 and at the time when Aggie's father, William John Swann was born they lived at 29 West Street, Corby (now known as Corby Glen) near Grantham. James Swann appears to have also had a shop at Ingoldsby. Aggie's father was born at Corby on 3 January 1859 and he had an older brother and a younger brother and sister who were also born at Corby.

The whole family emigrated in the early 1860s to New Zealand and two more boys were born. They moved again, this time to Fiji, where they arrived on 4 July 1867. They settled in Levuka on the island of Ovalau which was then the administrative centre of the Fiji Islands.

William returned for a short time to England to train as a chemist and, after a career as ship's apothecary in the South Seas, in 1889 he settled in Apia, Samoa where he established a chemist's shop.

He married a local girl, Pele and their first child, Margaret Pele was born on 29 July 1893. Agnes Genevieve (Aggie) was born on 31 October 1897 and a third daughter, Violet Mary on 31 August 1899.

In 1917 Aggie married a New Zealander, Gordon Hay-Mackenzie and after his death married Charles Grey, also a New Zealander.

Aggie founded Aggie's Hotel in Apia in 1935 and she soon became well-known throughout the South Seas for her hospitality. The business prospered during the Second World War, when American troops were quartered there and, after the war, the hotel became an important part of Western Samoa's, commercial and cultural life.

The remarkable esteem in which she was held was demonstrated when, in 1971, she became the first commoner to appear on a Samoan postage stamp. She was hostess to the Queen and Prince Philip during their visit in 1977 and in 1983 was the first Samoan to receive the Queen's Service Medal. She died in her hotel in Apia, Western Samoa, at the age of 90 in June 1988. An obituary in the *Daily Telegraph* of 29 June 1988 quoted James Michener as follows :

'I used to get over to British Samoa as often as I could, just to eat some decent food at Aggie Grey's Hotel ... It was always with a gasp of relief and a cry of joy at seeing dear Aggie

again. She was ebullient, efferves-cent, outrageous and terribly bright' ... Michener emphasises, however, that Aggie was not the original Bloody Mary 'But it was Aggie, and she alone, who fortified my writing in the editing stages, who remained as a visualisation of the island manipulator when the play was in formation, and who lives, in a curious way, as the real life Bloody Mary'

FURTHER READING

Eustis, *Aggie Grey of Samoa* (1979)

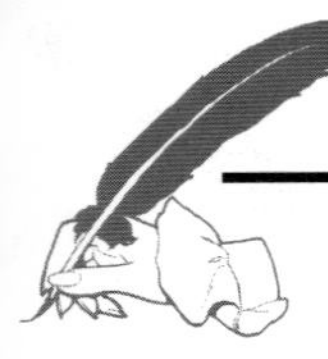

Eliza GUTCH

Folk-Lore Writer

Eliza Hutchinson, who was born in 1841 at Little Gonerby, near Grantham, was the eldest of the six children of Simon Hutchinson, a land agent. In 1868 at the age of twenty-seven Eliza married John James Gutch, a partner in a firm of solicitors in York, who was some thirty years her senior.

When the English Dialect Society was founded in 1873 of the 200 founder members Mrs Gutch, as she was always known, was listed as one of the eleven women. She was an active member and the annual reports record her work over a number of years in extracting and indexing 'provincialisms'.

In July 1881 her husband died and Mrs Gutch was left with "three youths and one girl". She continued with her work in collecting dialect words and folk-lore and the editor of the *English Dialect Dictionary* (Vol. I 1898), Dr Joseph Wright, included the name of Mrs Gutch amongst those who had assisted him in collecting material.

Mrs Gutch was a lady of many interests, including architecture, literature, education and assisted a number of charities. Over a period of seventy years she frequently had articles published under the pseudonym 'St. Swithin' in Notes and Queries. Mrs Gutch was the last surviving founder of the Folk Lore Society which was established in 1878 and, indeed, one of her 'St Swithin' contributions supported the suggestion which was taken up by others and eventually lead to the formation of that body.

Mrs Gutch is best known in Lincolnshire for her part in the production of Volume V of *County Folk-Lore, Printed Extracts No.VII. Examples of printed Folk-Lore concerning Lincolnshire (1908)* which is a 437 page collection of Lincolnshire folklore. It is divided into three parts, which are further subdivided into fifteen separate sections, entitled, 'natural or inorganic objects', animals', witchcraft', 'ceremonial', 'traditional narratives' and so on. The book is often known as 'Gutch and Peacock' because it was actually compiled by Mrs Gutch and Mabel Peacock (q.v.). The reason for the collaboration of these two ladies is probably because of Mrs Gutch's knowledge of south Lincolnshire and of Mabel's knowledge of the northern part of the county. It also appears that Mabel Peacock, although a greatly respected collector of folk-lore, preferred to write in collaboration with others.

When Mrs. Gutch died in March 1931 the Yorkshire Architectural Society recorded her passing as follows :

"We have lost by death this session the person of Mrs Gutch, our oldest member, she having joined the society in 1885, as a life member, dur-

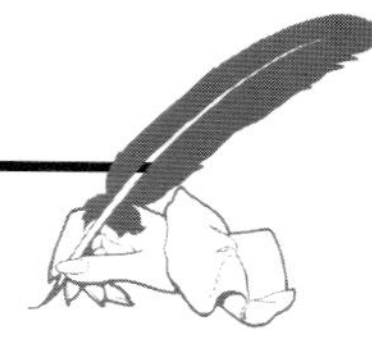

ing which time she showed extraordinarily keen interest in the Society, seldom missing a meeting, ready to maintain its fair name whenever that should be assailed, and fearlessly criticising in a friendly and helpful way any short-coming of those entrusted for the time being with the work and the furtherance of the Society. By her death the Society loses a staunch and enthusiastic member. She will be much missed and hard indeed to replace".

SOURCES

Elder, Eileen M. '..but who was Mrs Gutch' in *Newsletter* No 55 Society for Lincolnshire History and Archaeology January 1988 pp. 23-26.

Elder, Eileen M 'An Identity Revealed' in *Newsletter* No 64 Society for Lincolnshire History and Archaeology April 1990 p. 9-10 Society for Lincolnshire History and Archaeology.

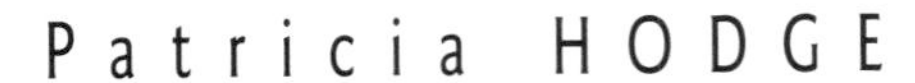

Patricia HODGE

Actress

Patricia Hodge was born in Cleethorpes in September, 1946 where her parents and aunt and uncle had bought a house in St. Peter's Avenue which they converted into a very successful hotel called 'The Berkely', renowned throughout Lincolnshire for serving wonderful teas even during post-war rationing. When she was four the hotel was sold and Patricia's father went to work for the local brewers, Hewitts, where he very quickly became their top manager and ultimately took over the running of their flagship, 'The Royal Hotel', in Grimsby. The family remained there until its compulsory closure in the mid 60s to make way for road redevelopment.

She attended St. Martin's Preparatory School and then Wintringham Girls Grammar School and at the age of 15 she went to St. Helen's School, Northwood, Middlesex as a boarder to study for her 'A' Levels. Patricia first came into contact with the entertainment world when stars appearing locally stayed at 'The Royal Hotel' and after a visit to a London theatre with her parents at the age of ten, decided that there was nothing she wanted to do more than go on to the stage. Patricia had studied piano from the age of six with Miss Kathleen Davis in Grimsby, ballet with Miss Florence Draper and elocution with Mrs. Carr and, as a result, she took part in many Lincolnshire festivals over a number of years.

Her first acting was in a school play at Wintringham and she continued whilst at St. Helens. But as a career in acting

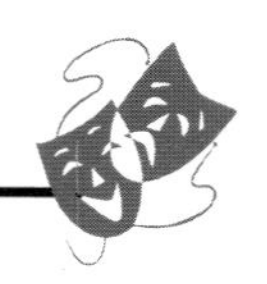

seemed out of the question at the time when she left school, she attended teachers training college. After teaching for a year she applied for a place at the London Academy of Music and Dramatic Art (LAMDA) and was accepted but was unable to get a grant. Determined not to miss the opportunity she worked as a Nanny during holidays, looking after, among others, Joseph Losey's son and Ian Holm's children.

Patricia won the Eveline Evans award for best actress on graduating. Her first West End appearance was at the Globe Theatre in 1972, a small part and understudy of the leading role in the musical version of *Rookery Nook*. The following year saw her on television, since when she has seldom been off the small screen, making her name in such popular series as *Rumpole of the Bailey, Jemima Shore Investigates, Hotel du Lac, The Life and Loves of a She Devil* and *The Legacy of Reginald Perrin*. Other television appearances in major drama include the ballet teacher in the *Naked Civil Servant*, Lady Diana Cooper in *Edward and Mrs. Simpson*, and in *The Death of the Heart*, and the Pinter-scripted *The Heart of the Day*.

Patricia's film credits Include co-starring with Jeremy Irons and Ben Kingsley in *Betrayal, The Elephant Man* with John Hurt; *Sunset* with Bruce Willis; *Thieves in the Night; Heavy Metal; The Waterloo Bridge Handicap; The Disappearance; Just Ask for Diamond* and, most recently, *The Leading Man* and the yet to be released *Prague Duet* and *Jilting Joe*.

Although Patricia's television and film career has kept her extremely busy she is essentially a theatre actress. In the West End she began her career with *Popkiss*, a musical, which was followed by *Two Gentlemen of Verona*, and then she was chosen by Bob Fosse to play the leading lady in his musical *Pippin*. Subsequently she played in *The Mitford Girls* in 1981 and *Noel and Gertie* in 1989 for both of which she was nominated for an Olivier Award. She has also performed in *Benefactors, As You Like it; Then And Now; A Little Night Music* at the Royal National Theatre; *The Prime of Miss Jean Brodie* at The Strand. *In Separate Tables* and *Shades*, both at the Albery Theatre, and most recently in David Hare's production of *Heartbreak House* at the Almeida.

Success has enabled Patricia to achieve her second ambition - to own a house after her upbringing in an hotel. Her talents are varied and she paints, renovates furniture and sews. She plays the piano and guitar and learned the ukulele for her role as Nancy Mitford at the Chichester Festival in 1981 in *The Mitford Girls*.

Patricia was delighted when, in July 1996, she was awarded an honorary doctorate of Hull University by Bishop Grossteste College, Lincoln. She is married to a musician and music plays an important part in her life. They have two sons now aged nine and six. It has often been said that Patricia Hodge is one of the rare breed of British actresses whose talents extend over the whole range of performance.

Annie HUTCHINSON

Puritan

Annie Hutchinson was born in 1591 and was the daughter of Francis Marbury, the master of Alford Grammar School and a priest. Her mother, Bridget Dryden was from a Northamptonshire Puritan family and a relative of the poet laureate, John Dryden. Annie was educated by her father and, not surprisingly, absorbed much of his independent spirit.

Francis Marbury was not slow in criticising the Church of England and by the age of 23 he had been imprisoned for his views three times. Eventually he was removed from his post as teacher and preacher. Revd Marbury was reinstated in 1594 by which time he had fourteen children to support and he felt obliged to suppress his own views and conform to the Established Church.

Francis Marbury's loyalty was rewarded by offer of the rectory of the fashionable London Church St. Martin's Vintry. Anne together with her parents, brothers and sisters moved to London in 1605.

In 1611 Anne's father died and in the following year William Hutchinson a clothier of Alford married Anne and she returned to live in her birthplace. Revd John Cotton's fame as a preacher at St Botolph's Church, Boston became known to them and William and Anne began making regular journey's to hear him. Cotton's belief in the purification of religious observance greatly influenced Anne and she began holding meetings in her own home for the women of the Alford area.

The views of John Cotton and his followers were tolerated under James I but Charles I was not so lenient. In 1633 a number of Puritans led by Cotton emigrated to America and joined the Pilgrims who had founded Plymouth Colony, Massachusetts in 1620. The Hutchinson's were not able to sail with Cotton because the birth of daughter Susanna was imminent. However, in the summer of 1634 Anne, William, and their ten children set sail for Boston, Massachusetts.

Anne soon became very popular and John Cotton wrote of her that she "did much good in our town" as a midwife and nurse. She held religious meetings for women in the home as she had done in England and these became so popular that husbands joined their wives and up to eighty people would gather in her house to hear Anne preach. She preached a unique theology which emphasised the role of faith.

As her fame spread people from neighbouring towns came to her meetings. But, perhaps inevitably, Anne began to make enemies and eventually a difference arose between her and John Cotton. The colony's leaders, including Cotton, felt threatened and a synod at Boston, Mass. on 30 August 1637 condemned her doctrines. In November 1637 she was tried and sentenced to banishment. In 1638 Anne and her husband settled on Rhode Island.

In 1642 William Hutchinson died and Annie moved to New York County, but soon afterwards she was murdered by Indians together with her servants and all but one of her children - a total of sixteen people. Her surviving son Edward was also murdered by Indians in 1675.

FURTHER READING

Battis, E. *Saints and Sectories : Annie Hutchinson and the Antinomian Controversy in the Massachusetts Bay Colony* (1962)

Jean INGELOW

Authoress

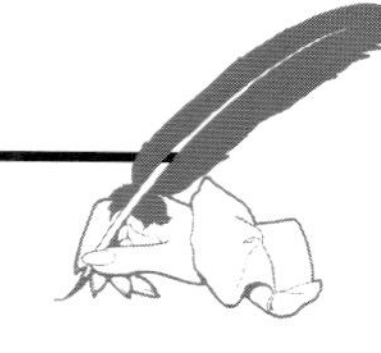

The Ingelows owned a bank in Boston which collapsed in 1825. The family moved to Ipswich after the bankruptcy but not before Jean was born in Boston on 17 March 1829. She was the first child of William and Jean Ingelow. They eventually had four daughters and four sons. The sons were taught by a local clergyman and the daughters by their mother.

Jean began writing verse and contributed to the *Youth's Magazine* and later became the editor. Although Jean never married, her early poems contain many references to an unhappy love affair. The family settled well in Suffolk, but they kept in touch with their cousins the Pyes, who lived in Louth. When the bank in Ipswich, for which Jean's father worked, collapsed the Ingelows moved again, this time to London. Jean was persuaded to publish a collection of poems and as a result *A Rhyming Chronicle of Incidents and Feelings* was published in 1850.

She wrote many poems and short stories, but it was not until 1863 that her second book *Poems* was published. This brought the comment from Alfred Tennyson 'Miss Ingelow, I do declare you do the trick better than I do'. The book went to no fewer than thirty editions. When Tennyson died in 1892, a petition was sent to Queen Victoria asking that Jean Ingelow be appointed poet laureate in his place, but presumably the Queen did not favour a female poet.

Jean Ingelow's most famous poem, *High Tide on the Coast of Lincolnshire 1571*, is still included in present day anthologies. Jean died on 20 July 1897 and a memorial window was placed in St. Botolph's Church, Boston.

FURTHER READING

Peters, M. *Jean Ingelow, Victoria Poetess* (1972)

Eliza JOYCE

Murderess

Eliza Joyce was the second wife of William Joyce, a gardener, and they lived in Boston. They appeared to have led a happy and prosperous married life. Eliza already had a daughter before marrying William and he had a son and daughter by his first marriage. Only the son, William junior had survived.

Fifteen year old William was a sickly boy and had been ill for some time when a doctor was called to see him on the 13 September 1842. By Friday the 16th he had improved considerably but when the doctor next called he found William ill again with violent stomach pains and sickness.

For a time William's health improved but he died a few days before Christmas. At the following Lincoln Spring Assizes Eliza Joyce was arraigned on a charge of murdering Edward William Joyce. Because the dead boy had been incorrectly called 'Edward' the indictment was found to be faulty and the case was transferred to the Summer Assizes. On the 18 July, 1843 Eliza again appeared in the dock, but the charge had been reduced to attempted murder. Eliza was acquitted.

William and Eliza Joyce separated. In June 1844 after she had been for some time an inmate of Boston workhouse Eliza confessed to Mr Sturdy, the workhouse master, that not only had she poisoned William but the two girls as well.

Eliza Joyce was tried at Lincoln on 18 July 1844 and pleaded guilty. The trial lasted less than an hour and she was executed at Lincoln Castle on 2 August 1844.

SOURCE
Lincoln, Rutland and Stamford Mercury 26 July 1844

Madge KENDAL

Actress

Margaret Shafto Robertson was born at Cleethorpes on 15 March 1849. Madge, as she was usually known, came from a family who had been connected with the stage for over two hundred years. Her great-great-grandfather, James Robertson, was a dramatist and actor and her grandfather, J. W. Robertson, was co-lessee of the Peterborough Theatre which was part of the Lincoln circuit. This included, in addition to Lincoln and Peterborough, Boston, Grantham, Grimsby, Huntingdon, Newark, Spalding, Grimsby and Wisbech. In each of these towns the Robertsons built a theatre. Madge's father, William Robertson, eventually became managing director of the company and he always had to be ready to play any part for which a suitable actor could not be found!

With such a background it is not surprising that Madge was attracted to the stage from a very early age. Her parents moved to London and, at the age of five, Madge played the part of Marie in *The Struggle for Gold*. This was followed by several other small parts. At the age of seven her mother took her to Bristol where the theatre was managed by a Mr Chute who had been an actor on the Lincoln circuit. Madge was given the part of Eva in *Uncle Tom's Cabin* at the Bristol theatre and she sang four songs. Madge remained in Bath and attended Miss Pillinger's Music Academy. At the age of fifteen she sang in burlesque at Bradford and went on to sing for six weeks at the Haymarket Theatre, London.

In 1863 she played in *A Midsummer Night's Dream* at the reopening of the Theatre Royal, Bath. This was the first of many appearances she made with Ellen Terry who was then aged sixteen and was to become a close friend. On 29 July 1865 Madge played Ophelia in Hamlet at the Haymarket Theatre and other Shakespearean roles followed in quick succession. By the age of twenty-one she had acted over fifty parts in productions ranging from Shakespeare to pantomime.

In 1869 Madge married the actor-manager William Hunter Kendal, with whom she appeared in many productions. Possibly the highlight of Madge Kendal's career was her American tour on which she was accompanied by her husband. Such a long journey was at that time regarded as a somewhat hazardous enterprise and a farewell banquet was held at the Hotel Metropole on 16 July 1889 under the chairmanship of the Rt. Hon. Joseph Chamberlain, MP at which about 200 well-known people were present. The tour was a great success but unfortunately Madge in her autobiography is very sparing with dates.

Although Madge and her husband partnered each other in many

notable productions and were a popular duo William was always overshadowed by his wife. However, they were regarded as an ideal partnership both on the stage and in their private lives which did much to raise the status of the acting profession. The Kendal's had two sons and three daughters and retired from the stage in 1908. William died in 1917.

Madge Kendal was appointed a Dame Commander of the British Empire (DBE) in 1926 and in the following year was awarded the Order of the Grand Cross (GBE.) In 1932 Dame Madge Kendal was granted the Freedom of Grimsby.

Her autobiography, *Dame Madge Kendal by Herself* was published in 1933 and she died on 14 September 1935.

Mary LEFFEY

Murderess

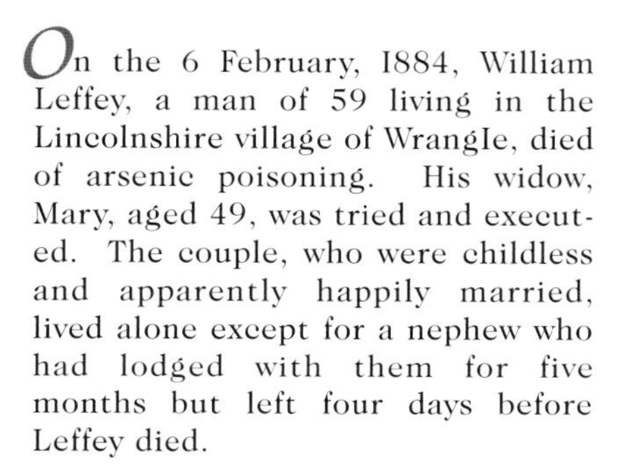

On the 6 February, 1884, William Leffey, a man of 59 living in the Lincolnshire village of Wrangle, died of arsenic poisoning. His widow, Mary, aged 49, was tried and executed. The couple, who were childless and apparently happily married, lived alone except for a nephew who had lodged with them for five months but left four days before Leffey died.

At the trial evidence was given by eleven inhabitants of Wrangle who confirmed that Mary Leffey travelled frequently to Boston to sell butter. Early on 6 February she travelled as usual with Samuel Spence, the local carrier. Her husband travelled with her for half an hour and then walked home.

At about three that afternoon Leffey staggered to the home of Dr Bubb, the Wrangle surgeon, and when he discovered that the doctor was out he asked to see Miss Bubb. When she appeared , Leffey produced a basin about half full of rice pudding and told her that he had been poisoned by it. When Dr Faskally, who was acting as *locum*, returned, after examining Leffey, he arranged for him to be taken home and put to bed.

When Mary Leffey returned home from Boston she went upstairs but was told by her husband to go back downstairs and he didn't want to see her any more. Leffey died at nine o'clock in the presence of several villagers. Two days later Mary was charged with poisoning her husband with arsenic and the trial took place at Lincoln Assizes on 7 May when she pleaded 'not guilty'. Evidence was given that the remains of the rice pudding contained the enormous quantity of 135 1/2 grains of arsenic. Two grains is a fatal dose and the pudding must have originally contained enough arsenic to kill over a hundred adults!

Although evidence was given by the defence of several suicide attempts by Leffey, after 35 minutes, the jury found Mary guilty and she was subsequently executed.

SOURCE
Lincoln, Rutland and Stamford Mercury 9 May 1884

Daphne LEDWARD

Gardener

Daphne Ledward has long since become a naturalised 'yellow-belly' having lived in the 'forgotten county' since 1954. Her affection for the county is such that she becomes very irritated with those who regard it as flat and uninteresting. Daphne and her husband live in a thatched cottage in the fenland of south Lincolnshire. Her husband, John, was a BBC engineer and they met when she was working on *Gardeners' Question Time!*

Daphne was actually born in Bradford 'during the last air raid on Yorkshire towards the end of the Second World War'. Her father and mother were both BBC engineers and moved to Essex when Daphne was aged three. The family moved to Lincolnshire in time for Daphne to receive most of her education at Stamford Girls' High School. She left school before sitting for 'A' levels in order to train as a quantity surveyor but the training she received, which she describes as consisting of instruction in 'how to get ten cups of tea (at the same time) out of a two cup teapot', led her to decide that a career move was desirable. So she became a welfare assistant with the now defunct Kesteven County Council. It was at this time that Daphne developed her interest in writing and was successful in getting a number of heartrending short stories published in *Valentine and Mirabelle* which brought in much needed pocket money.

When Social Services were reorganised, although she was by then head of the department, she became uneasy and, in 1972, she left to become a landscape gardener. In 1980 BBC Radio Lincolnshire invited Daphne to do a gardening slot and two years later she joined Radio 4's *Gardeners' Question Time* she says 'as the token woman'. She presented and helped to produce *Gardeners' Direct Line* for BBC 1 from 1982 until 1990 and worked on satellite television's *Sky by Day* from 1988 until 1991.

After the death of Percy Thrower in 1988 Daphne joined Radio 2 as *Jimmy Young's Gardener*. In 1994, along with other members of the *Gardeners' Question Time* team.

Having now stopped working for Classic FM Daphne continues to work for Radio 2, Radio Lincolnshire and Granada Television's *Goodlife* gardening programme as well as writing for several magazines including *Gardeners' World*. She has written or co-written eleven books and she is at the time of writing (May 1998) working on another two. The latest, *A Kitchen Garden Year Book* which includes art work by South Lincolnshire Artist Freda Ward and photographs by Daphne's husband, is to be published in July, 1998. Daphne is very popular with the gardening fraternity because of her down to earth practical approach whether on the radio, television or in her writing.

Daphne also works as a landscape designer and garden consultant and enjoys lecturing and judging. She says that she has also been known to 'sit in shops and garden centres handing out verbal largesse and making an ass of myself at garden shows'. Obviously for such a busy person 'spare-time' must be very limited but whenever possible she goes sailing and caravaning and she does occasionally find time to work in her own garden at the cottage and in a large field about three miles away!

Ethel Lillie MAJOR

Murderess

Ethel and Arthur Major lived in a council bungalow at Kirkby-on-Bain and their marriage was reasonably happy. But after a neighbour told Arthur that a young girl who had been brought up as Ethel's sister was in fact her daughter the marriage deteriorated and for the next five years there were violent quarrels.

The Majors had a son, Laurence, who had been born in 1919, who said that his father came home drunk nearly every night. He and his mother would often have to sleep in a hut in the garden or on a couch in his grandfather's tiny cottage.

In 1931 Ethel took out a summons for separation and maintenance, but did not proceed with it when Arthur promised to reform. In fact matters did not significantly improve. At the beginning of May, 1934, three weeks before Arthur's death, Ethel found letters signed 'Your loving sweetheart, Rose' in her husband's jacket pocket. Ethel told her doctor and a sanitary inspector that she suspected that the letters were written by her neighbour. There were a number of embarrassing incidents and on 22 May Arthur got home from work at five o'clock and prepared his own supper. Later that evening he collapsed in great pain and his wife and son helped him to bed. When Ethel's father called later that evening he found Arthur speechless with agony his legs jerking and foam coming from his mouth. A doctor eventually arrived and diagnosed an epileptic fit. Medicine was administered and Ethel and Laurence went to bed leaving Arthur still foaming at the mouth. The sick man remained alone until Ethel took him a cup of tea at half-past seven next morning and Arthur lay in a stupor all that day. When the doctor called he thought Arthur was much better and Ethel went shopping. In the evening the convulsions returned and Arthur died in great agony on 24 May some forty-eight hours after first falling ill.

By midnight that day Ethel had contacted the undertaker and arranged the funeral but the doctor had not been called. When the doctor was eventually contacted he wrote a certificate saying that Arthur Major aged 44 had died of '*status epilepticus*'. Two days later, while Ethel and the relatives were preparing to go to the funeral, a police inspector came to say it must be cancelled and it appeared that an anonymous letter had started police investigations.

Ethel was arrested and tried at Lincoln in 1934. At an autopsy it was proved that Arthur had eaten corned beef which contained strychnine for his supper on 22 May and probably a second dose was administered while he was ill in bed. On 31 October, 1934 the jury found Ethel guilty of murder, adding a strong recommendation to mercy but she was executed at Hull on 19 December 1934.

SOURCES
Lincolnshire Echo 29, 30, 31 October 1934,
1 November 1934

Kathleen MAJOR

Historian

Kathleen Major is the daughter of George and Gertrude Major and was born in London on 10 April 1906. She was educated at several private schools before going up to St Hilda's College, Oxford. Miss Major's first research interest was in the Medieval Boroughs and when she came to choose a subject for her B.Litt. she intended to extend this work but instead it was suggested to her by Professor Powicke that she collect and edit the *Acta* of Archbishop Stephen Langton. This was the foundation of her interest in ecclesiastical documents which was to be of great importance for the future study of the Diocesan Records for the See of Lincoln.

The work of collecting material for the *Acta* involved a systematic tour of cathedral libraries and archives at a time when access to such records was not easy and working conditions far from ideal. However, the people she met and the work involved in tracing elusive papers was an invaluable foundation on which to build her future work. Miss Major first met Canon Foster the founder of the Lincoln Record Society when she went to Lincoln in connection with her work on Langton's *Acta*. Soon after her thesis was submitted in 1931 she was asked to become co-editor with Foster of the *Registrum Antiquissimum of the Cathedral Church of Lincoln*. In the same year she was appointed Librarian of St Hilda's College and when, in 1936, the Lincoln Diocesan Record Office was established Miss Major became the first full-time archivist.

In 1945 Kathleen Major was elected to a Lectureship in Diplomatic at Oxford and three years later she was promoted to Reader. In 1955 she became Principal of St Hilda's College Oxford where she remained until 1965. In 1966 she was appointed a part-time Professor of History at Nottingham University relinquishing this appointment in 1971.

During a very busy academic life Miss Major continued with her work on the *Registrum* first in conjunction with Canon Foster and after his death in 1935 she continued this work until the final volume was published in 1973. She was General Editor from 1935 until 1975 for the Lincoln Record Society and edited the first series of Lincoln Minster Pamphlets which were published by the Friends of Lincoln Cathedral from 1948 until 1956. Kathleen Major has had many articles and reviews published in the academic press. In 1933 she published *A short account of the Church of St Mary Magdalen, Gedney* and in 1937 the first volume of the *Registrum* (Vol. iv) edited entirely by Miss Major was published and further volumes followed in 1940 (Vol. v), 1950 (vi), 1953 (Vol. vii) 1958 (Vol. viii), 1968 (Vol. ix), and 1970 (Vol. x). In 1950 her *Acta Stephani Langton...* was published by the Canterbury and York Society and in the same year *A short account of All Saint's Church, Holbeach* was published together with a revised edition of Miss Major's earlier work on Gedney Church.

Since returning to Lincoln Miss Major has spent much time, together with Stanley Jones and Joan Varley on the preparation of a *Survey of Ancient Houses in Lincoln* which is a series of faciscules published by the Lincoln Civic Trust.

Every student of the Lincoln Diocesan Records owes much to Miss Major's published material but there are also the indexes and catalogues prepared by her without which work by present day historians would be much more difficult.

Mary Anne MILNER

Murderess

On 20 July 1847 Mary Anne Milner of Barnetby le Wold appeared at Lincoln Assizes on a charge of murdering her mother-in-law. Both Mr and Mrs Milner senior showed evidence of poisoning and an autopsy on Mrs Milner disclosed arsenical poisoning.

There was no proof of who had administered the poison and the jury found Mary not guilty. However, she was immediately put on trial for the murder of Hannah Jickels.

Hannah Jickels was a neighbour of Mary Ann Milner and her child had died on 15 June with many of the symptoms of having been poisoned. Before Mrs Jickels died on 26 June she was able to make a statement that she was taken ill after having eaten pancakes prepared by Mary Milner. A surgeon from Brigg was able to analyse remains of the pancakes and he estimated that Mrs Jickels had been given 30 grains of arsenic.

A very full account of the trial was published in a broadsheet and Mary Ann Milner was found guilty and sentenced to death by hanging. In those days a hanging was a social occasion. On this occasion the crowd that had gathered at Lincoln Castle on 30 July 1847 were told that Mary had hanged herself with a handkerchief in her cell during the night.

Henry William, the Deputy Under Sheriff of Lincolnshire reported the incident to Sir George Grey, Chancellor of the Duchy of Lancaster, as follows :

'It is a matter to be regretted, considering what has happened in this instance, that it has never been the custom in the Gaol of this County to keep watch on the convicted criminals sentenced to death in such manner as I believe is usual in Newgate and other prisons and, therefore, as the Keeper of the prison and the Chaplain have informed they neither of them observed anything in the conduct or demeanour of the convict which gave occasion to excite the slightest suspicion of any intention on her part to commit suicide. She was left according to the usual custom alone in her cell.

This event will, however, occasion the adoption by the Authorities of the County Prison of such measures as will prevent the recurrence of a similar one in the future'.

As a result of this incident it was ordered that, in future, all condemned prisoners were to have two warders in attendance until execution.

SOURCES
Lincoln, Rutland and Stamford Mercury 23 July 1847

I am grateful for information communicated by Jane Briggs, of the Friends of Lincoln Castle.

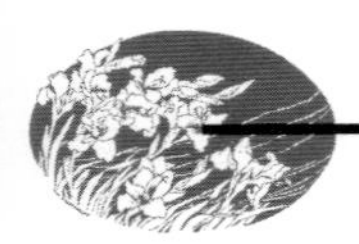

Flora MURRAY

Rural Community Council

Flora Murray came to Lincolnshire for her first job in 1935. Although proud of her Scottish ancestry, she was born at Leeds in Yorkshire. After graduating with a London University Honours B.Sc(Econ.) degree from the University College of Hull (as it then was) in 1934 she became the first administrative assistant with the Lindsey Rural Community Council of which the Headquarters was the then National Council of Social Science. In 1939 Miss Murray became assistant secretary and when the Director, Major North Coates, OBE, M.C., died in 1957 she was appointed in his place. Being Chief Officer to the Rural Community Council included the administration of its associated bodies, the number of which increased greatly during Miss Murray's service and the Council extended to become Lindsey and Holland Rural Community Council covering the area from the Humber to the Wash.

The work of the Community Council was very varied as its aim was to foster every aspect of county life including the support of rural industries, the provision of village halls, the assistance of Parish Councils, the encouragement of Adult Education and the provision of facilities for music and health education, which last included keep fit classes. It was the Community Council which initiated the Lindsey Local History Society with the support of Canon Foster, Mr Tom Baker and many other distinguished historians.

When the Rural Community Council set up the Lindsey Standing Conference of Voluntary Youth organisations in 1943 Flora as its Honorary Secretary represented the Community Council on the County Youth Committee. In 1943 work for playing fields was also included and Miss Murray acted as honorary secretary for the Lindsey, Lincoln and Grimsby Playing Fields Association and the Holland Playing Fields Association. This work for the promotion of sport in Lincolnshire was recognised in 1970 when the Duke of Edinburgh, as President of the national Playing Fields Association, presented Miss Murray with his certificate at a ceremony at Buckingham Palace.

In 1950 the Community Council organised a Lincolnshire Conference which led to the setting up of County Old People's Welfare Committees. The Rural Community Council was asked to administer this work and the Lincolnshire Physically Handicapped Association was started by the Rural Community Council in 1955.

The Rural Community Council also helped to establish the county Association of Young Farmer's Clubs, the Lincolnshire Trust for Nature Conservation and the Lincolnshire Association for the Arts. The latter body took over the Local History Society's Collection of Bygones and used them to form the basis for the Museum of Lincolnshire Life.

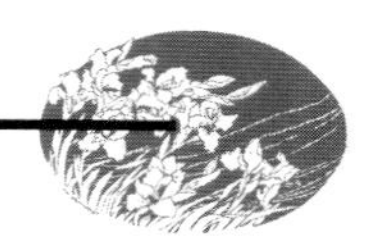

In 1956 the Rural Community Council established and thereafter administered the Lincolnshire Branch of the Council for the Preservation of Rural England and in 1968 the Lincolnshire Historic Buildings Joint Committee which was composed of representatives from the various bodies concerned with the built heritage of the county.

In 1972 Miss Murray's outstanding and dedicated work for the Community Council for over thirty-seven years was recognised by the award of an OBE and when she retired in 1974, on the re-organisation of local government, a presentation was made to her by the Bishop of Lincoln on behalf of the Council and many organisations she had assisted.

After retirement Miss Murray has continued to work for people in many ways; with Age Concern, St Andrew's-with-Newland United Reform Church and Lincoln Civic Trust in particular. Flora has a life-long interest in local history and still works for the Society for Lincolnshire History and Archaeology. Her work over many years and in many capacities for S.L.H.A. was recognised when, after serving as its Chairman, she was elected a vice-president and by the award of honorary life-membership.

Flora's work for the rural community of Lincolnshire was recognised in 1990 by her old College, now the University of Hull, which awarded her an honorary M.A.

Dorothy OWEN

Historian

Dorothy Owen has been engaged for over forty years with Lincolnshire local studies. For ten years of that long period her work was with the Lincolnshire Archives Office, with the Lincoln Record Society and with the two societies which merged in 1974 to form the Society for Lincolnshire History and Archaeology.

Dorothy Williamson was born in 1920 at Hyde, Cheshire and her early education was at the Grammar School in that town. She went up to Manchester University in 1938 and graduated with first class honours in history in 1941. Dorothy then spent four years teaching history, Latin and French at Pontefract Girls' High School and then returned to Manchester University to undertake two years research on the medieval church.

Dorothy's first introduction to Lincolnshire came in July 1948 when she was appointed assistant archivist at the Lincolnshire Archives Office soon after it was first established. Her colleagues were Mrs. Joan Varley, who was the archivist, and the first of a succession of school leavers.

Dorothy became editor of the *Reports and Papers of the Lincolnshire Architecture and Architectural Society* which work she continued until 1964. As well as contributing to the Annual Reports of the Archives Office, which detailed deposits and the contribution being made to county historical studies, in 1956 Dorothy wrote The *Muniments of the Dean and Chapter of Lincoln* which was No. 8 in the series of Minster Pamphlets published by the Friends of Lincoln Cathedral under the editorship of Miss Major.

Amongst the many visitors to the Archives was Arthur Owen (a Lincolnshire man) whom Dorothy married in 1958. Although Dorothy and Arthur worked away from Lincolnshire until their retirement they continued their association with the county and their friends there.

In the intervening period Dorothy held several interesting archivist posts; Deputy Archivist at Lambeth Palace Library, archivist for the Bishops' Records and those of the Cathedral at Ely, and finally Keeper of the Cambridge University Archives in 1978. She also worked for the Canterbury and York Society and the British Records Association.

Dorothy also found time to publish several notable works of national and Lincolnshire interest, namely *Church and Society in Medieval Lincolnshire* in 1971 and *The Handlist of the Records of the Bishop and Archdeacon of Ely*. In 1988 she produced the invaluable *Handlist to Cambridge University Archives*, and delivered the Sandars Lectures in Bibliography on *The Medieval Canon Law : Teaching, Literature and Transmission* which were published in 1990.

On retirement Dorothy and Arthur returned to Lincolnshire and continued to contribute much to historical

studies. Dorothy edited the publications of the Lincoln Record Society until 1996 and was President of the Society for Lincolnshire History and Archaeology for ten years until 1997, as well as serving for a considerable number of years on the History of Lincolnshire Committee. Dorothy edited and contributed to works on ecclesiastical history, including a volume of specially commissioned studies entitled *A History of Lincoln Minster*.

In 1968 Dorothy was elected a fellow of Wolfson College Cambridge (and remains an emeritus fellow), and in 1985 Cambridge University conferred the degree of Doctor of Literature on her in recognition of her published contributions to historical research. Further recognition of her work came in 1995 with the publication of *Medieval Ecclesiastical Studies in Honour of Dorothy M Owen*, which contains a bibliography of her work.

In 1996 Dr Dorothy Owen was appointed to Membership of the Order of the British Empire.

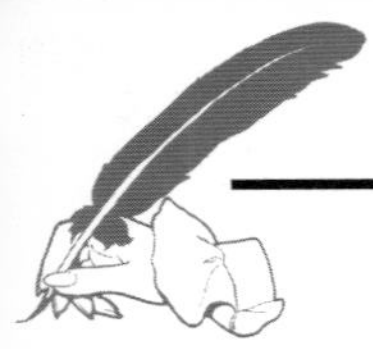

Mabel PEACOCK

Folk-Lore Writer

Mabel Geraldine Woodruffe Peacock was born at Bottesford Manor in North Lincolnshire, on the 9 May 1856. She was the second of the seven children born to Edward and Lucy Peacock between 1855 and 1863. The early education of the children was undertaken at home by their mother and Mabel and her elder sister Florence were sent to school in Edinburgh to complete their education. All of the Peacock children grew up with a love of the countryside and Mabel became a competent naturalist. Her brother Adrian became an outstanding botanist .

From an early age Mabel was expected to assist her father in his antiquarian studies. In 1873 she accompanied him to Holland, and later in the same year to London acting as his research assistant. In 1874 the second edition of *The Army Lists of the Roundheads and Cavaliers containing the names of the officers in the Royal and Parliamentary Armies of 1642* was published under the names of Florence and Mabel, who were aged nineteen and eighteen years respectively. Edward Peacock's diary clearly indicates that it was the work of his two elder daughters; though undertaken under his supervision.

At about the same time Mabel began to participate in the study of Lincolnshire dialect which was one of her father's interests and this, together with the study of folklore, were her main interests for the remainder of her life.

Edward Peacock gave up farming in 1874 believing that he could support his family by writing and by his investments. Although he had by this stage three novels and several other books to his credit this was not to be.

However, Mabel and her sister Florence established reputations as writers of short articles, book reviews and verse. Mabel wrote *Tales and Rhymes in the Lindsey Folk-Speech* in conjunction with her brother Max and this was published in 1886. Mabel and Max also wrote *Tales Fra Linkisheere* (1889) and *Lincolnshire Folk-Tales* (1897). On her own account Mabel wrote *Lincolnshire Rhymes and Verses* (1907) and she contributed many articles to the *Journal* of the Folk-Lore Society and to *Lincolnshire Notes and Queries* and other publications.

In 1887 Mabel's mother died and she had increased domestic responsibilities but she still continued to write. By 1892 Edward Peacock was heavily in debt and he had to sell a large part of his extensive library and many other valuable items. In the summer of that year he and his two daughters moved to Dunstan House in Kirton Lindsey.

One of Mabel's best known works which she produced in collaboration with Mrs Gutch *(q.v.)* is Volume V of

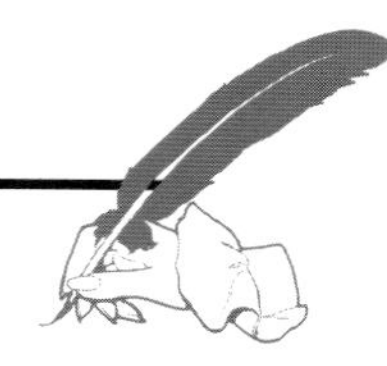

County Folk-Lore, Printed Extracts No.VII. Examples of printed Folk-Lore concerning Lincolnshire (1908) which is a 437 page collection of Lincolnshire folklore.

Mabel earned the respect of the many scholars who visited her father in connection with his academic interests. Her nephew, Thomas Peacock who was the younger son Mabel's brother Adrian, when writing about a visit to his aunt in 1910 described her as follows :

"Aunt Mabel was a most impressive and unusual person, short and thick set with short dark hair - a most unusual style for a woman in those days- Her speech was very deliberate with a roll of the R due to her Scottish education. She had a sense of humour but it was not sparkling and witty as was her sister-in-law. Aunt Kitty. Her general demeanour was rather sad and serious as if she felt life had been unkind to her."

Following the death of her sister Florence in 1900 Mabel alone had the responsibilities of running the household and caring for her ageing father. At the end of 1901 they moved into the smaller, more economical Wickentree House, a short distance away.

Edward Peacock died in 1915 and Mabel on 17 July 1920. She was buried in Grayingham churchyard where her brother Adrian was then rector. He died two years later and was buried beside her. There was a considerable collection of Lincolnshire folklore and dialect material which remained unpublished at the time of Mabel's early death.

It is difficult in a comparatively brief account to convey adequately the academic and personal characteristics of Mabel Peacock but clearly anyone interested in Lincolnshire's Heritage owes much to the Peacock family.

FURTHER READING

Robert Pacey *Fragments of a Lincolnshire Friendship - Letters from Mabel Peacock to John Ostler Nicholson* (1989) unpaginated

Eileen Elder 'Edward Peacock and his Family : an Introduction to the Peacocks, Collectors of North Lincolnshire Dialect from 1850 to 1920' in C. Sturman (ed.) *Some Historians of Lincolnshire* (1992) pp 70 to 81

Eileen Elder editor and compiler *The Peacock Word Books 1884-1920* Scunthorpe Museum Society (1997) pp. 3 - 21.

Julie PEASGOOD

Actress

Julie Peasgood comes from a Grimsby family who have long been associated with the entertainment business. Pearl Peasgood, Julie's mother, ran away from her Grantham home at the age of eighteen to join Bertram Mills circus. Pearl became a tight rope walker, an equilibrist and a magician's assistant. She even allowed herself to be sawn in half! With such a background it is not surprising that, when Julie first announced that she wanted to be a dancer she received active support from her parents.

Julie was educated at Wintringham Grammar School and in 1968 won a Royal Academy of Dancing Scholarship which entitled her to two free lessons each week at the nearest RAD centre. It says much for Julie's determination that she was prepared to set off at 5 a.m. in order to catch the milk train to York for her lessons! It was well worth while as in 1970 Julie won a place at the Arts Educational School in London. In 1973 a foot injury put a sudden end to any hope Julie had of following a career in dancing. Fortunately, in 1974, she was selected from over sixty applicants to play the lead in *Cherryripe and the Lugworm Digger* which was the first in the series *Seven Faces of Woman* broadcast by London Weekend Television.

Since this first appearance Julie has taken part in thirty-eight television productions including *Taggart, Boon, September Song, First born, This Year Next Year* and Carla Lane's *Luv*. She had Barry Grant's baby in *Brookside!* Julie's most recent television part was Jo Steadman the motor bike riding tax inspector in *Emmerdale*.

In the theatre Julie worked with the Royal Shakespeare Company at Manchester's Royal Exchange and the Old Vic. She has appeared in a total of nineteen stage productions including Shakespeare, Dickens and Shaw.

Julie was one of the Team Captains in the 1997 television series *Give us a Clue* and was regular television critic for the BBC on *Good Morning with Anne and Nick*. She has hosted the Radio travel show *The Great Escape* and presented Channel 4's *For Love or Money*. Most recently Julie has stood in for Judy Finnegan in Granada's *This Morning*. She has also appeared in two films, *The House of the Long Shadows* and *The Lake*.

Joan PLOWRIGHT

Actress

Joan Plowright was born at Brigg on 28 October 1929 and is the daughter of Daisy Margaret and William Ernest Plowright. Her brother David Ernest was born a year later. Joan was educated at Scunthorpe Grammar School, the Leban Art of Movement Studio and the Old Vic Theatre School.

After graduation she joined George Devine's English Stage Company and her first stage appearance was in *If Four Walls Told* at the Croydon Repertory Theatre in 1948. In 1952 she went to South Africa on her first overseas tour. Joan's first London appearance was in *The Duenna* at the Westminster Theatre in 1954. In 1956 she became a member of the English Stage Company at the Royal Court Theatre, London. It was here that she met Laurence Olivier who she married in 1961.

Particularly notable performances were as Jean Price in Osborne's 1957 production of *The Entertainer* and Wesker's *Roots* in 1959. At the Chichester Festival's inaugural season in 1962 Joan was acclaimed for her performances as *Saint Joan* in Shaw's play and as Sonya in her husband's production of *Uncle Vanya*.

She repeated these roles for the National Theatre in 1964 and received the Evening Standard's Best Actress Award for *St. Joan*. She was leading actress for the National Theatre Company for ten years and played opposite Laurence Olivier as Portia in the *Merchant of Venice*, Masha in *Three Sisters*, Sonya in *Uncle Vanya* and Hilde Wangel in The *Master Builder*.

Joan's many successes in the West End include performances in Zeffirelli's productions of *Saturday Sunday Monday* and *Filumena* at the Globe Theatre from 1974 until 1978. During 1986 and 1987 she appeared in *The Seagull* and *Bed Before Yesterday* at the Lyric Theatre and *The House of Bernard Alba* The Globe.

On Broadway Joan has played in *The Entertainer, The Chairs, A Taste of Honey* and *Filumena* and has won The Tony, The New York Critics' Circle Award and The Newspaper Guild of New York Award for Best Actress.

Joan's more recent television appearances include Meg in Harold Pinter's *The Birthday Party*, Lady Bracknell in *The Importance of Being Ernest* and Peggy in *And the Nightingale Sang*. In 1993 she appeared in *Stalin* for which she won a Golden Globe Award and a Emmy Nomination.

Joan's first film was *The Entertainer* which she made in 1960 and in 1976 she made her first film for television which was *The Merchant of Venice*. In 1988 she won the Film Actress of the Year Variety Club Award for her performances in Peter Greenaway's *Drowning by Numbers* and Beryl Bainbridge's film version of her novel

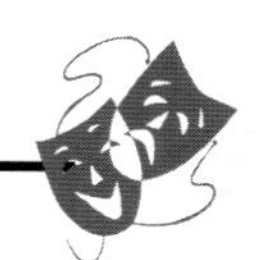

The Dressmaker. Recent films include *I Love You to Death* with Kelvin Kline and *Dennis* with Walter Matthau, *101 Dalmations* with Glenn Close, *Widows Peak* with Mia Farrow and *Jane Eyre* with William Hurt.

Although best known as a talented classical actress Joan Plowright is also an accomplished stage director.

Lady Olivier was awarded the CBE in 1970 and is a member of the R.A.D.A Council. She is a vice-president of the National Youth Theatre and lists her recreations as reading, music and entertaining.

Lord and Lady Olivier had three children; Richard who is now a director and writer, Julie Kate and Tamsin who are both actresses. They are a very close family and meet whenever possible. Lord Olivier died in 1989.

Su POLLARD

Actress, Singer

Although Su Pollard was actually born in Nottingham in 1949 she told me she has "spent quite a bit of my life in Lincolnshire particularly since my parents came to live in the county over twenty years ago:. It was whilst at the Peveril Secondary School in Nottingham that she was first introduced to acting by taking part in school plays and pantomime. Su says "At the age of ten my drama teacher arranged for me to audition for Co-operative Arts Theatre in Nottingham and this was my introduction to serious acting".

"My family took our annual holidays at Mablethorpe and it was there at the old open air Dunes Theatre that I won my very first stage prize in a junior singing contest at the age of ten coming first singing *Bobby's Girl*". This early success encouraged Su to learn as much as possible about acting and theatre life and she jumped at the chance to appear on the Television Show, *Opportunity Knocks*. I am sure many readers will remember this long running talent spotting show presented by Hughie Green. Su came second to a singing Jack Russell dog!

"That experience of the big time made my mind up as to what I wanted to do in life and I packed my bags and went to stay with my aunt in London". After she had registered with Equity and found an Agent offers soon came along and she found that her eleven years experience with the Co-operative Arts Theatre had given her the background which enabled her to take part in all types of plays. She was offered and accepted a number of national tours including *The Desert Song, Rose Marie, Godspell, and Grease*.

These were followed by Not Now Darling, Oh Mr. Porter and a play written by and starring Andrew Sachs called *Philately Will Get You Nowhere*. More recently Su has toured in the musical *Babes in Arms* with Mathew Kelly, played the role of Sally in *Me and My Girl* and toured with *See How They Run*. Su has appeared in numerous radio programmes, has made guest appearances on a number of television shows and she is particularly proud to have taken part in five *Royal Variety Shows*. Su also has to her credit a CD entitled *Among Friends* and she has made a single *Starting Together* which reached number two in the charts. Her first album, *Su*, went silver. One of the highlights of Su's very varied career was her debut at the Royal Festival Hall when she sang with the BBC Radio Orchestra. Sue also created the role of Suzette in the hugely successful farce *"Don't Dress for Dinner"* in the West End and New Zealand with late great Simon Cadell.

To most of us Su is best known for her role as Peggy in *Hi-De-Hi* for BBC television which ran for nine series and this made her one of our best loved comedy actresses. This series was followed by *You Rang M'Lord* in

which she played Ivy and the most recent series *Oh, Dr Beeching*. Her popularity and versatility were recognised in 1989 when she was the subject of *This is Your Life*.

Su leads an extremely busy life and she told me that she looks forward to returning to stay with her parents and relaxing in rural Lincolnshire whenever possible. She particularly enjoys Lincolnshire's own fish and chips which she fetches from the shop round the corner. I'm told by the local Vicar that she also enjoys going round with a bucket and extracting money from the bystanders at the local church fete!

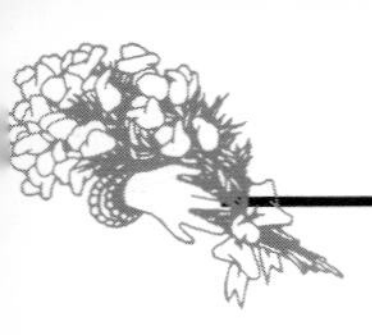

Norma PROCTER

Concert Singer

Norma Procter was born in Cleethorpes in 1928 and comes from a musical family. Her earliest memory is of standing on the kitchen table when she was three years old singing children's hymns which she had learnt at Sunday School. At the age of five, Norma began having piano and singing lessons and these continued until the age of thirteen when education had to take priority. After leaving school three years later Norma worked as a nurse/secretary to an ophthalmic surgeon until her singing career was established.

From an early age Norma sang in the Methodist Churches at Scartho and at Mill Road, Cleethorpes and competed successfully in Music Festivals throughout the county. In 1946 she sang for the first time in *Messiah* during a Christmas performance at Mill Road Church. After singing 'He was despised' she realised what a wonderful message music had to give to the world. It was at this point that she quietly decided to dedicate her life to God's glorious gift of music and singing.

After hearing Kathleen Ferrier's unforgettable interpretation of 'He was despised' during a performance of the *Messiah* by Grimsby Philharmonic, Norma asked the singer to autograph her new copy of *Messiah* - a Christmas present from her mother. Kathleen was very kind and told Norma to come and say 'hello' on her next visit to Grimsby. After several visits Norma asked Kathleen about teaching and she recommended her own Professor Roy Henderson writing his address on the back of the envelope which had contained her fee for the concert of 25 guineas !

Norma auditioned with Roy Henderson in January 1947 and he asked her to move to London. She preferred to travel each week from Grimsby for a lesson and she is grateful that the excellent train services which existed at that time enabled her to live in her home town for the whole of her career.

'Prof.' as he was always known was Norma's only vocal teacher. At his suggestion she studied musicianship and piano with Alec Redshaw in Cleethorpes. Norma says her success as a singer was due to her 'Prof.' and Alec Redshaw together with Hans Oppenheim with whom she studied German Lieder and, later, Paul Hamburger.

After a year with 'Prof.' working only on basic techniques, Norma sang in the Glyndebourne Chorus at the Edinburgh Festival Seasons of 1948 and 1949 - she knew then that Opera would never be her first love. Throughout her life Kathleen Ferrier continued to encourage Norma, and even attended her London debut at Southwark Cathedral in 1948.

As Norma became known she was in demand all over the UK and eventually across the Continent, and she made

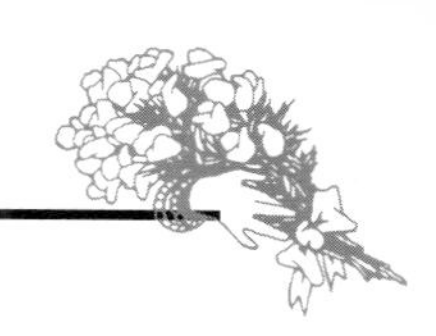

many notable recordings and broadcasts. Her first broadcast was live and started at 8.30 a.m.! Among her particular memories are her tours on the Continent and to Israel and South America.

In 1959 Norma sang Lucretia in Britten's *Rape of Lucretia* at the Aldburgh Festival - a role she repeated again in 1960. In January 1961 she made her Covent Garden debut singing the title role in Gluck's *Orpheus* wearing Kathleen Ferrier's comforting robe from her last performance eight years before during many long rehearsals. Norma again realised opera was definitely not her *forte*, but she enjoyed singing *Orpheus* concert performances on many occasions later.

Among the many colleagues she met during her career Norma found Dame Joan Sutherland especially kind and helpful and, as with Kathleen, they shared some wonderful laughs together! One of her closest colleagues and friends was the lovely, late Jennifer Vyvyan and another was the kindly, encouraging, Heddle Nash and Norma's first unforgettable *Dream of Gerontius* with him. Another colleague was Webster Booth who began singing as a chorister at Lincoln Cathedral but there are so many more to whom Norma would like to pay special tribute. Sadly space does not allow further individual names.

Of the many conductors with whom she worked each has his own special memory for Norma. She remembers the kindness of Sir Malcolm Sargent, the great Lincolnshire born conductor, and his wonderful orchestral arrangement of her beloved Brahms' *Four Serious Songs*. Norma also remembers particularly sharing his last London Concert with Bruno Walter. It was he, with Kathleen and Sir Peter Pears, who first introduced her to Mahler in the very moving *Das Lied von der Erde*. Mahler became one of Norma's best loved composers with especially memorable conductors - Bernard Haitink, Rafael Kubelik, Bernstein, Horenstein and many others.

Norma was always happiest singing in churches and cathedrals especially in the early days when no applause was allowed. Lincoln Cathedral takes first pride of place, and she also remembers in particular Westminster Abbey, where she sang whilst it was still in its Coronation splendour. Her favourite London Concert Hall was the Albert Hall and she remembers with particular pleasure taking part in the 1974 *Last Night of the Proms*. On the Continent 'The Golden Hall' of the Musikverein in Vienna, the Concertgebouw in Amsterdam, the Teatro Real in Madrid and Palacia de Musica in Barcelona were among many other favourite venues.

Norma acknowledges the help and encouragement of many people in their several ways including fellow singers, conductors and accompa-

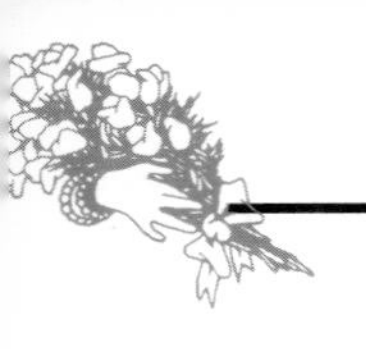

nists, and also her brother-in-law, Norman, who drove her many hundreds of miles. It is impossible to do justice to Norma's achievements in a short article and she humbly thanks all those unnamed friends and colleagues for their inspiration, encouragement and support throughout her thirty-five year career.

In the 1960s Norma accepted Alec Redshaw's invitation to become President of the Grimsby Philharmonic Society although in name only, and in 1974 she was made an Honorary Member of the Royal Academy of Music. She quietly retired in 1983, a mortal and emotional blow for any singer or performer, and, although she missed her singing, she did not miss living out of a suitcase and the hazards of modern travel! She later began teaching with accompanist and friend Anne Holmes and also the occasional Master Class and Jury Member.

Norma received many compliments and 'thank you's' during her career but she says "...perhaps the one I love most came from a Northern Committee member, who told their President "Bye, it were worth a Bring-and-Buy Sale to 'ave 'er!"

Lucy ROBERTS

Polar Explorer

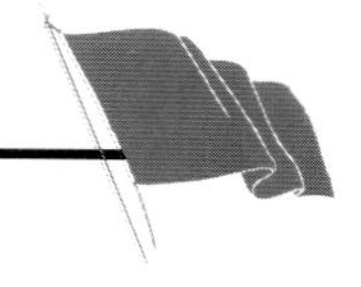

Lucy Roberts was born in Lincoln in 1968 and attended St Mary's Preparatory School before moving on to Roedean School. She went up to Stirling University to read for a BA Honours degree in Political Studies.

After a post-graduate degree course in journalism she became a reporter on a trade magazine, *Interior Design*. In June 1991 Lucy became an assistant editor on *The Review* which specialised in international reinsurance. In 1994 she was promoted to run the title and became one of the Company's youngest ever editors. During this period she also initiated and launched a new title: *International Risk Management*.

In February 1993 Lucy moved to the business desk on the *Independent* newspaper and became the editor of the City Diary column. It was whilst she was editing City Diary that she met and interviewed Caroline Hamilton whose dream it was to walk to the North Pole. Lucy decided she would quite like to go as well! Although Lucy had spent time on expeditions on the South Downs, the New Forest and the Lake District whilst working through the various stages of the Duke of Edinburgh's award and always had a passion for being outdoors she is not a keen walker for its own sake. There has to be a goal to reach and the North Pole seemed the perfect challenge!

Her late brother, Simon, was also a real inspiration. He was into walking in a big way and whilst at Gordonstoun ran the Mountain Rescue Team. When he died Lucy realised how important it was to her to try and achieve as much out of life as possible. She has run marathons in New York and London and competed in the first London Triathlon in 1997.

Following a rigorous selection procedure, Lucy was chosen from 600 hopefuls to become part of a team of 20 British women to attempt the first ever Polar relay. The expedition, the McVities Penguin Polar Relay 1997, enabled five groups of four women to walk in relay to the North Pole. Lucy was a member of the fifth and final team which, after covering 230km in ten days, finally reached the Pole on 27 May 1997 to become the first British women to reach the North Pole.

Only two women of different nationalities had ever reached the North Pole before, as a party of mixed teams using dogs and skidmobiles.

Despite being stuck at the North Pole for six days Lucy plans to revisit the Pole - only this time she has to walk all the way, The aim of the second expedition entitled 'Girls on Top' in 1999, along with a fellow team member, is to be one of the first British women to walk all the way to the Pole.

In 1998 she hopes to complete the 54 mile Comrades run in South Africa to raise money for her local church. Lucy was elected Woman of the Year in 1997 and she says that if it was not for her mother's support and encouragement she could not have achieved so much.

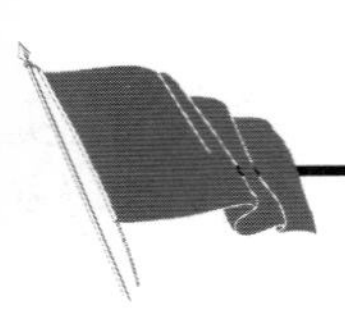

Ethel RUDKIN

Antiquarian

Mrs Ethel Rudkin was born in 1893 and, after she was widowed during World War I, she made her cottages at Willoughton, and later at Toynton All Saints, places of pilgrimage for a growing number of researchers, several of whom became distinguished in their own fields, who were interested in the past of Lincolnshire which was at that time a very neglected county. Whether they were interested in pre-historic sites or deserted medieval settlements they could be sure that Ethel Rudkin would know in which direction to point them.

"Peter" Rudkin as she was generally known was a dedicated field-worker whose knowledge was shared with everybody. She had a unique relationship with the agricultural community and farmers would bring her their finds which they had ploughed up. These country people were a good source of information about old implements, traditional sayings and folk-lore.

In 1936 she published Lincolnshire Folklore and in March 1984 she was presented with the Cooke Lake Medal for Folklore Research. Ethel discovered and investigated an important medieval pottery industry at Toynton and one of the joys of visiting her was to see the rows of complete jugs from that site which are now in the City and County Museum, Lincoln. The great flood of 1953 exposed on the Lincolnshire coast remains of an early salt industry and, of course, it was Ethel Rudkin who was on hand to record this.

She was a lone figure in the 1920s but her collaborators grew in numbers, especially after the war, and she was held in high esteem by archaeologists and historians of all ages and experience. A conversation, an encounter in the home, an expedition into the field, a group discussion, always stimulated her enquiring mind and so often was the occasion for original ideas to emerge that led others, motivated by them, to follow new lines of research. So wide was her interest that few among her large circle of friends missed this exciting experience.

1934 Ethel appealed in the *Lincolnshire Magazine* for bygones, both agricultural and domestic, to form a museum. Major North Coates, then head of the Rural Community Council which administered the Lincolnshire Local History Society, supported the idea and material of all types, large and small, flowed into Ethel's stores. So, in embryo, was born the Museum of Lincolnshire Life which was founded at the Old Barracks in Burton Road, Lincoln and opened to the public in 1969. A plaque outside the museum eloquently describes Mrs Rudkin's long and dedicated service to this cause, as Honorary Research Secretary of the Lincolnshire Local History Society.

Her final years were absorbed in the

study of salt production and pottery manufacture. So much so that she moved from her beloved Willoughton to live in Toynton All Saints among the kilns she so lovingly excavated in a field known as "The Roses". This produced a great range of medieval pottery and the hope was often expressed that this great industry in the South Wolds would one day be more fully appreciated and understood.

Throughout her long life Ethel inspired many to follow her example. Young enthusiasts and more serious students were welcomed to her home and received the same kind reception.

Ethel Rudkin died on 21 September 1984 at the age of 92 two weeks before the publication of a volume of essays in her honour entitled *A Prospect of Lincolnshire* which covered the range of her contributions to the archaeology, history, folklore and dialect of the county.

Joyce SKINNER

Educationalist

Joyce Skinner was born on 5 September 1920 in 'down-hill' Lincoln at 33 Drake Street off Carholme Road and is the daughter of Matthew and Ruth Eva Skinner. Joyce's early education was at St Faith's Primary School and Christ's Hospital Girls' High School. She went up to Somerville College, Oxford to read History graduating BA in 1941 and obtained her MA in 1945. She taught first at Bridlington Girls' School from 1942 until 1945 when she joined the staff of the Perse Girls' School in Cambridge. In 1950 Joyce moved on to Keswick School where she remained until she took up a lectureship at Homerton Teacher Training College, Cambridge in 1952.

In 1955 she was appointed visiting Professor of Queens College, New York for one year, returning to Homerton in 1956 becoming deputy principal of that College in 1960. In 1964 the opportunity arose for Joyce to move back to Lincoln as Principal of Bishop Grossteste College. During her time at the College it became co-educational and it established its first degree in education with the University of Nottingham. A critical shortage of teachers led to the establishment of two outposts for mature students; one at Grimsby and one at Scunthorpe and Joyce was also responsible for introducing an in-service programme for serving teachers. The College itself also expanded considerably at this time and a new Library, Students' Union and Senior Common Room were built.

In 1971 Joyce was appointed a member of the Curriculum and Development Advisory team for the Government of Kenya and in the same year she was awarded an Honorary Fellowship of the College of Preceptors. In 1974 she was appointed Director of the Cambridge Institute of Education and was also elected to a Fellowship at Hughes Hall, Cambridge. Joyce's service to education was recognised in 1975 when she was appointed a Commander of the Order of the British Empire (CBE). In 1979 Joyce became academic secretary of the Universities' Council for the Education of Teachers and she remained in that post until her retirement in 1984 when she returned to live in Lincoln.

In 1989 Joyce was awarded an honorary Doctorate of Education by the Council for National Academic Awards and in 1997 an Honorary Doctorate of Letters by the University of Hull.

During much of her career in education Joyce served on bodies representing the interests of teachers. For seventeen years she served on the executive of the Association of Teachers in Colleges and Departments of Education and was chairman of that body during the year 1967/8. She served on the

Lincoln City Education Committee from 1964 until 1974 and on Cambridgeshire Education Committee from 1974 until 1980. She also served for a number of years on the Advisory Committee for the Supply and Education of Teachers.

Since her retirement Joyce has returned to live in Lincoln and leads a very busy life but when she has time her recreations are walking, reading and conversation.

In 1989 Joyce and her sister Edna Purchase published an account which they had written for Edna's grandchildren of their life in 'downhill' Lincoln up to the time of leaving school. This is a particularly articulate and evocative story of those growing-up in the years immediately before the Second World War.

FURTHER READING

Skinner, J. and Purchase, E. Growing-Up Downhill (1989)

Doris STOKES

Medium

Doris Sutton was born in 1920 at Grantham and was a weak, sickly baby. She described her childhood as "unhappy and confused," largely because from an early age she was plagued by mysterious voices in her head.

She first visited a medium at the age of 13 and at the seance her dead father came through to her. Doris did not become a medium herself until she was 24 when she was invited to a spiritualist church after the death of her infant son.

Perhaps, in part, because of her ordinariness, Doris Stokes became a highly successful medium and travelled the world with her roadshow, *An Audience with Doris Stokes*. She appeared on stage sitting in a chintz armchair with a simple flower display beside it, she wore studiously dowdy frocks and a permanently waved hairdo, and invariably addressed her audiences (for the most part female and inclined to tears) as "lovey" and "dear." Having warmed them up with a few jokes about sexual practices in the afterlife, she regaled them with a flood of "messages" - usually on domestic subjects (dining suites, garage doors) - from such dead relations as "Uncle Wilf" and "Auntie Dot."

Doris's popularity was such that when she went to Australia the massive Sydney Opera House was packed for three nights in a row and a private plane was hired to take her from city to city. Even a T.V. soap opera was postponed to make way for her! When she had been raised by American television to the status of a "spiritualist superstar," she had much contact with dead celebrities (particularly John Lennon and Elvis Presley), and made extensive use of the medium of tabloid newspapers. Her followers included Ronnie Kray and Derek Jameson and Doris claimed to have helped the police with a number of murder inquiries. Unfortunately the police forces concerned denied this.

Her first book *Voices in My Ear* was published in 1980 and five more followed. Their combined sales reached two million. She claimed to have visited "the Other Side" and said that its denizens "were not floating around in white sheets or sitting on clouds strumming a golden harp."

She said that the "voices ... just spill out of my mouth and I don't know what I'm saying half the time. I suppose I'm a bit like a telephone exchange."

In fact, Doris spent many hours on the telephone speaking to the bereaved, parents of murdered children and relatives of accident victims. Eventually she rarely left her home and the telephone was her main link with the world outside.

For many years Doris Stokes wrote an immensely successful agony column for *Chat* magazine which brought in

an enormous volume of correspondence. Doris suffered a long series of operations and she often joked that she was being "taken over bit by bit". Often she told of her father's advice to her "Cast your bread on the waters with love and it will come back buttered".

Doris became known as "the Gracie Fields of the psychic world." After much suffering she passed over to the other side at the age 68 in 1987. She left behind her husband John, a faith healer and adopted son Terry a bus-driver and part-time psychic.

Copyright Grantham Journal

Sarah SWIFT

Nursing Pioneer

Sarah Anne Swift was born on 22 November 1854 at Kirton Skeldyke. She was the daughter of a family who had farmed at Blossom Hall Farm from the mid-eighteenth century. However, the family appears to have moved from Kirton in the mid-nineteenth century to the Red House at Donington Wykes, where Sarah spent her childhood.

In 1877 Sarah, after completing her education at the Cowley School in Donington, entered the Dundee Royal Infirmary as a probationer nurse and completed her training on 31 October 1879. She was appointed Assistant Matron of the Dundee Home for Incurables and remained there until 1886. In 1887 she was Ward Superintendent of the City Infirmary, Liverpool and in 1888 and 1889 Night Superintendent of the London Fever Hospital. She then decided to study nursing in the United States of America before accepting the post of Superintendent of Nursing at the British Seamen's Hospital in Constantinople, returning to England in 1890. In December of that year she entered Guy's Hospital as a 'Lady pupil'. This was because, at that time, nurses were divided into two groups - a small body of lady pupils and a larger number of other nurses. The lady pupils usually came from well-to-do homes, were well educated and paid a considerable fee for their training.

After completing her training Sarah was appointed Assistant Matron at Guy's and Lady Superintendent of Guy's Trained Nurses Institute which was an institute for private nurses with its headquarters in St. Thomas' Street. In 1900 Sarah Swift was appointed Matron, a post which she held until her retirement in 1909.

However, Sarah Swift's retirement did not last long and her nursing experience was called on at the outbreak of war in 1914, when she was appointed Matron-in-Chief of the Joint War Committee of the British Red Cross Society and the Order of St. John. She was responsible for the nursing in 1,786 auxiliary hospitals and under her guidance 4,730 trained nurses were employed. An additional 762 nurses were trained for service in war hospitals in France and Belgium and 6,666 were despatched to other fronts, making a total of 7,428.

In 1916 Dame Sarah Swift was the driving force behind the establishment of the College of Nursing which in 1946 became the Royal College of Nursing with its own Coat-of-Arms and the motto *Tradismus Lampada* (We hand on the Torch).

Sarah Swift was awarded the Royal Red Cross (First Class) and also the Order of the British Empire. She was created a Lady of Grace of St. John of Jerusalem and finally in 1919 she was created Dame Grand Cross of the British Empire.

Dame Sarah Swift died in London on 27 June 1937 at the age of 83. As a memorial to her the floor of the Lady Chapel in Kirton Parish Church was repaved and a tablet erected together with the illuminated address which had been presented to Dame Sarah by the British Red Cross.

FURTHER READING

Bowman, Gerald *The Lamp and the Book - The story of the Royal College of Nursing 1916-1966* (1967)

Katherine SWYNFORD

Duchess of Lancaster

Katherine Swynford was born in 1350 and was the younger daughter of Sir Payne de Roet a knight from Hainault who had come to England to serve Edward III as Guienne king of arms. Katherine's older sister, Phillippa, married Geoffrey Chaucer who was one of the king's esquires and she became a lady of the queen's bed-chamber.

Katherine married, in about 1367, Sir Hugh Swynford who had manors at Coleby and Kettlethorpe and was in the service of John of Gaunt, Duke of Lancaster. They had one son, Thomas, and Katherine became lady-in-waiting to John of Gaunt's wife, Blanche. Blanche died in 1368 and was the subject of a book by Geoffrey Chaucer entitled *The Boke of the Duchesse*. Katherine was appointed governess of Gaunt's two daughter's, Phillipa and Elizabeth, and appears to have become his mistress soon after the death of her husband, Sir Hugh, in 1372.

John of Gaunt's second wife, Constance of Castile, died in 1394 and on 13 January 1396 he married Katherine in Lincoln Cathedral. In the following year their children, John Beaufort, Earl of Somerset; Henry Beaufort, Bishop of Winchester; Thomas Beaufort, Duke of Exeter and Joan Neville, Countess of Westmoreland were declared legitimate except for the succession to the throne. The Beaufort family were to play a leading part in the politics of fifteenth century England and through her son, John, Katherine was great-great-grandmother of Henry VII, the first of the Tudor monarchs.

Katherine died on 10 May 1403 and was buried in Lincoln Cathedral. A chantry had been refounded in 1437 by Katherine's daughter Joan for the welfare of the souls of her various Beaufort and Lancastrian kinsmen. Joan was buried at the side of her mother in the chantry chapel but it was severely damaged during the Civil War. The tombs were moved to their present position later in the seventeenth century.

FURTHER READING

Goodman, A. *Katherine Swynford* (Lincoln 1994)
Seton, Anya *Katherine*

Margaret Thatcher

Prime Minister

Britain's first woman Prime Minster was born in Grantham on 13 October 1925 and is the daughter of the late Alfred and Beatrice Roberts. Her father kept a grocer's shop and he was a Methodist local preacher and a member of the local council. The family lived above the shop in North Parade. On 3 September 1930 Margaret Hilda Roberts became a pupil at the local county school and at the age of ten years and six months she won a scholarship to Kesteven and Grantham Girls' School.

She became interested in chemistry and decided to sit the entrance examination for admission to Somerville College, Oxford. Her friend, Margaret Goodrich, the daughter of Canon Goodrich vicar of Corby Glen was already an undergraduate at Lady Margaret Hall. If she was to be successful Margaret needed to learn Latin and her father employed the classics master at the King's School to teach her. She was unsuccessful in the 1942 entrance examination, which she sat in her fourth term in the sixth form, but was accepted in 1943.

From the very beginning Margaret joined the Oxford University Conservative Association and in her last year at Oxford she became the first woman undergraduate to be elected chairman of the Association. At the 1945 general election she canvassed for the Conservatives in Oxford and in Grantham. At meetings she would often address the audiences before the candidate. In 1947, after having graduated with the degree of Bachelor of Science, she started work as a research chemist with the plastics firm British Xylonite at their works in Manningtree, Essex, with a salary of £350 a year.

In early 1949 she was adopted as the Conservative candidate for the Dartford constituency, becoming at the age of 23 the youngest woman candidate in the country. Soon after, she moved to the research department of J. Lyons & Company in Hammersmith and obtained lodgings in Dartford. She was defeated at the 1950 election and moved to her own flat in Pimlico but stood again for the same constituency in the 1951 election and was again defeated.

Margaret Roberts had met Denis Thatcher whilst living in Dartford and they married in 1951. She now left full-time employment so that she could study law. In 1953 the twins, Carol and Mark, were born and in 1954 Mrs. Thatcher was called to the bar. She decided to specialise in tax law and practised for five years until, in 1958, she was adopted as the Conservative candidate for the Finchley constituency. She was elected at the 1959 general election and remained the Member of Parliament for Finchley for the whole of her career in the House of Commons. In 1961 she was appointed Joint Parliamentary Secretary to the

Minister of Pensions and National Insurance and remained there until the defeat of the Conservative Government in 1964.

On the election of a Conservative Government in 1970, Margaret Thatcher was appointed Secretary of State for Education and Science, a post she held until the Government was again defeated in 1974. She was elected leader of the Conservative Party in 1975 and when the Conservatives regained power in 1979 she became Prime Minister. She remained in that office until her leadership was challenged and in November, 1990 she was succeeded by John Major. Mrs Thatcher remained on the Back Benches until the end of that Parliament but did not stand for parliament in the next general election, going to the Lords in 1992 as Baroness Thatcher of Kesteven. Her husband, Denis, was created a Baronet in 1990. No Prime Minister has remained in office for a longer period since Lord Liverpool in the first quarter of the last century. During her eleven years in office she established a personal political philosophy, popularly spoken of as 'Thatcherism' based on a mixture of values gained during her formative years and the resolution to persevere with political policies despite objections from her critics and doubts among her supporters.

Lady Thatcher was awarded two of the highest honours anyone in this country can receive: the Order of Merit in 1990 and the Garter in 1995. She is also a Fellow of the Royal Society.

Lady Thatcher lists her recreations as going to the opera, walking, gardening and reading.

FURTHER READING

Thatcher, M. The Downing Street Years (1993)

Thatcher, M. The Path to Power (1995)

Sybil THORNDIKE

Actress

Dame Sybil Thorndike was born in Gainsborough on 24 October 1882 and was the eldest of the four children of Revd. Arthur Thorndike and his wife Agnes Bowers. Her father was appointed a minor canon of Rochester Cathedral before Sybil was two years old and the family left Lincolnshire. Sybil and her brother Russell from a very early age showed great interest in amateur dramatics and by the age of four Sybil performed at family gatherings. By the age of seven they had written and performed their own play entitled *The Dentist's Chair* which had the sub-title *Saw their silly heads off!*

When Russell went away to school Sybil turned from acting to the piano, which she played at Sunday School. At the age of eleven she played Beethoven at a London Concert but the theatre was not altogether forgotten. Sybil still performed in plays at her school and was in demand for local amateur productions.

Her parents expected her to make a career as a concert pianist but a painful left wrist ruled this out and she auditioned unsuccessfully as a singer. Finally in 1903 Sybil and Russell auditioned for admission to 'Ben Greet's Academy', which had been founded as an acting school in 1896.

Sybil's parents agreed that she should join the Greet Company on an American tour in 1904 and thus her early acting career was established. Full details of the numerous plays, films and television productions are recorded in Sheridan Morley's biography.

Clearly Dame Sybil's Lincolnshire roots can have had little if any influence on her but it is nice to know that one of this country's greatest actresses was born in the county.

Dame Sybil Thorndike died on 9 June 1976.

FURTHER READING

Morley, Sheridan *Sybil Thorndike : A Life in the Theatre* (1977)

Joan (Franklin) VARLEY

Archivist

Joan Varley was born on 8 November 1904 in Southampton, as the second child of Mr and Mrs Franklin. Her elder brother, Archie, is an Anglican priest who was for many years a curate in the parish of Portsea Island (Portsmouth). Joan was educated at the Southampton High School for girls, and then at the University College, Aberystwyth. Here she was taught history by Cecil Jane who tried in vain to improve her hand-writing, and she heard and performed (she was then a pianist) a lot of music. At that time Walford Davis organised musical education in the college. She took a first in history in the examinations of the University of Wales, and followed it by a diploma in education.

She also became engaged to marry her contemporary W J (Bill) Varley, a Yorkshireman who was a pupil of the geographer H J Fleure, through whose influence he developed a strong interest in archaeology. Bill began his teaching career at the Chester diocesan teachers' training college, while Joan went to teach in the Llandudno Grammar School, before they married and settled near Chester. After some time Bill moved to an assistant lectureship in geography at Liverpool University and they lived in a flat in a Georgian house in the very centre of the city. They were already in thrall to a red cocker spaniel, Robin, who lived until at least 1944.

Joan took an active part in Bill's excavations, especially in the hill forts of the Welsh marches, and so came to know many young archaeologists such as Brian and Helen O'Neil, Jacqueline and Christopher Hawkes, and Gordon Childe, as well as Bill's pupils many of whom became archaeologists, like Margaret Jones and her husband Tom.

At the beginning of the second world war Bill disappeared into military service and Joan was absorbed by a censorship unit which was organised by Mrs Montsarrat, whose staff were almost all associated with Liverpool University. She continued to live in the house they had acquired at Frodsham in the Wirral; the marriage ended in divorce in 1947.

Joan had been drawn by Professor J A Twemlow, the palaeographer, into an editorial project which was eventually published by the Chetham Society (the Middlewich Cartulary). When the war ended she became Miss Major's successor as Lincoln diocesan archivist, and on the foundation of the Lincolnshire Archives Office in July 1948 became the archivist of the new committee which provided an archive service for Lincoln City, Lindsey, Holland and Kesteven County Councils. She eventually retired in 1972.

Joan had been joint secretary of the local branch of the Historical Association, and she edited the *Lincolnshire Historian* for the Lindsey and Lincolnshire Local

History Society until its absorption in the new Society for Lincolnshire History and Archaeology. In later retirement she took an active part in the surveys of medieval houses produced by the Civic Trust. She was always an active Soroptimist, and a member of the Federation of University Women and the Friends of Lincoln Cathedral, for whom she edited the second series of cathedral pamphlets.

SOURCE
Used with the permission of the author, Dr. Dorothy Owen.

Susanna WESLEY

Mother of the Wesley Brothers

Susanna Annesley was born in London on 20 January 1669. Her father had been vicar of the large parish of St Giles but, because of his Nonconformist tendencies, had been forced to resign his living. He later became the minister of the Puritan meeting-house of Little St Helen's, Bishopsgate.

On 12 November 1688 at the age of nineteen Susanna married Samuel Wesley who, then aged twenty-six, was a deacon in the Church of England at Bromley. Although both of them came from strongly Non-conformist families before their marriage they had returned to the Church of England. Samuel became priest of St Andrew's, Holborn in February of the year after their marriage but moved to Lincolnshire in June 1690 when he became rector of South Ormsby. The long association of the Wesley's with Epworth began in 1695 when Samuel became Rector of that parish.

It is believed that the Wesley's had nineteen children, ten of whom died before they were two years old. Susanna taught her large family herself and was very strict with them. The three surviving sons, Samuel, John and Charles were born in 1690, 1703 and 1707 and six daughters survived into adulthood. From the age of five the children had lessons for six hours each day. At six in the evening, as soon as family prayer was over, the children had their supper and were then washed, and they were put to bed by eight o'clock.

Susanna was a stronger character than her husband and a devoted mother who had considerable influence on her offspring. She was independent and clear-headed and not afraid to criticise and disagree with her husband at a time when women were expected to remain silent.

Samuel was not popular with his parishioners because of his High Church practices and his royalist sympathies. He was a man of strong views on morality and religion and was fearless in expressing his opinions regardless of the consequences. His parishioners burned his crops and injured his cattle. At an election in 1705 his life was threatened. One of the parishioners demanded the repayment of a debt but Samuel couldn't pay and he was imprisoned in Lincoln Castle. Susanna was left with little money to feed her family but she sent Samuel the few items of jewellery that she had so that he could feed himself. Fortunately the Archbishop of York intervened and paid a personal visit to Epworth leaving money to feed the family.

A fire at the rectory in 1709, which is believed to have been deliberately started, destroyed the rectory. All the family escaped except John

who was trapped in the top floor nursery. He was saved by jumping from a window into the arms of a neighbour who stood on the back of another. Ever since, to his mother, he was 'a brand plucked from the burning' a term which John often used to describe himself in later years. Susanna believed he had been saved for some great purpose and she wrote in her diary 'I do intend to be more particularly careful of the soul of this child, that Thou has so mercifully provided for'.

When it is realised that Susanna was bearing children for some twenty years it is amazing that she managed to teach her children, conduct her household with little domestic help, manage the tithe and glebe lands and her parish duties so cheerfully. In fact, it could only be done by a strictly enforced timetable. It has been said that the childhood piety of John Wesley was 'constructed on the principle of a railroad time table'. One of Susanna's grandsons said that 'She had the happy talent of imbuing a child's mind with every kind of useful knowledge in such a way as to stamp it indelibly on the memory'.

Samuel Wesley died in 1735 and Susanna lived for short periods with members of the family before finally leaving Epworth after 38 years to settle with John in London. She died on 23 July 1742 and was buried in Bunhill Fields near to John Bunyan and Isaac Watts. Susanna is remembered particularly for having given to Christianity her sons John, the preacher and founder of Methodism, and Charles, the writer of many of the best known of our hymns.

FURTHER READING

Harmon, R. H. *Susanna, mother of the Wesleys* (1968).

Katherine WILLOUGHBY

Duchess of Suffolk

Katherine (or Catherine) Willoughby was born in 1520 at Parham Old Hall, Suffolk, the only child of William de Eresby and Maria de Salinas, one of Catherine of Aragon's Spanish loyal ladies in waiting. Her father died in 1528 and she became the ward of Charles Brandon, Duke of Suffolk. He was a favourite of Henry VIII's and was at that time married to Henry's beloved youngest sister Mary. However, Mary suffered from a delicate constitution and in 1533 she died. Later that year, in September, Charles married for the third time and Katherine became Duchess of Suffolk, the title by which she was consequently known throughout her life even when a dowager and remarried.

The Suffolks made their country home in Lincolnshire at Grimsthorpe and Tattershall. They had extensive estates in the County through the Willoughby connection and through rewards for Charles's role in suppressing the pro-Catholic uprising the Pilgrimage of Grace in 1536. Katherine, although born a Catholic, was by now forming her own, Protestant, views on religion and was influencing her husband. She was strongly influenced by the preaching of Hugh Latimer at court, and at home the Suffolks had two openly Protestant preachers as their private chaplains. Katherine was therefore well suited for friendship with Henry VIII's sixth wife, Catherine Parr, who shared her religious views. In 1547 Catherine Parr published a Protestant religious pamphlet at the instigation of the Duchess of Suffolk.

In 1545 Charles Brandon died leaving Katherine with their two sons to bring up. Their education had been progressing well and they went up to Cambridge in 1549. The now Duke of Suffolk was of an age to be considered for a dynastic marriage however, and his mother wrote to her long-time friend and Lincolnshire neighbour, William Cecil, to prevent a match that did not allow the couple "to choose by their own liking". Tragically, on July 16th 1551, within hours of each other, both her sons died of the sweating sickness that had swept Cambridge that summer.

Katherine, whilst devastated at this double loss, continued to run her estates and sought to settle the remaining legal issues left from her husband's will. A Master Bertie, one of her Gentleman Ushers, was mentioned by her as acting on her behalf in June 1552. Richard Bertie was a steadfast Protestant and he and Katherine shared a mutual friend in Hugh Latimer, who officiated at their wedding in 1553.

Mary Tudor was now on the throne, and as staunch Protestants, the Berties were in real danger. Hugh Latimer was martyred amongst others known to them and Stephen Gardiner (the Lord Chancellor) was a powerful enemy. The family fled to the Continent and thence to Poland,

Katherine with a baby daughter in arms and giving birth to a son, Peregrine, en route. Their exile lasted until Elizabeth's accession in 1558 and they could return. Thomas Deloney wrote a ballad *The most rare and excellent history of the Duchess of Suffolk and her husband Richard Bertie's calamity* and in the early 17th century a play was also written about their plight.

Under Elizabeth I Katherine hoped for great religious reforms. She was always forthright about her religious views, pushing for religious services to be simple, clear of dogma, and in a language the people could understand. She found Elizabeth and her counsellors too conservative in this respect, and often wrote to William Cecil gently castigating him for this.

Her latter years were occupied with her children's marriages, fighting successfully for her daughter's husband's right to hold the title Earl of Kent, and seeing her son marry Lady Anne Vere (the Earl of Oxford's sister) for love, despite his mother's misgivings about the match. Katherine died in 1580, too soon to see her children happily settled with her grandchildren.

Katherine Willoughby's life spanned the 16th century and her religious views underwent changes from being born a Catholic to becoming a convinced and proselytising Protestant. She had two happy marriages, to two very different men, and her views on marriage for her children seem positively enlightened by the standards of the time. As one biographer puts it "in an age where women were to be seen and not heard, she was seen for her beauty and heard for her intelligence, wit, her spiritual integrity and zeal".

FURTHER READING

Read, Evelyn *Catherine, Duchess of Suffolk : a portrait* (1962)

Catherine WILSON

Murderess

Catherine Wilson was a native of Boston where she was housekeeper to Captain Mawer, an elderly master mariner. She appears to have been a widow but no trace of her husband has been found. The captain made a will leaving all his possessions to his housekeeper and died in October 1854 after ten days of violent diarrhoea and vomiting. It was noticed he was always worse after drinking tea his housekeeper had prepared.

Catherine moved to London and became the mistress of a young man called James Dixon. In December 1855 they took lodgings with Mrs Maria Soames in Bloomsbury. In June 1856 a doctor was called to treat Dixon, who was suffering from what was diagnosed as rheumatic fever. Dixon died two days later but Catherine continued to lodge with Mrs Soames.

When Mrs Soames was away on holiday the house was burgled and Catherine claimed that a box of her possessions had disappeared together with silver belonging to Mrs Soames. Catherine ingratiated herself with Mrs Soames and wheedled a considerable amount of money from her 'friend'. So much so that Mrs Soames on 15 October 1856 in desperation visited her brother, Samuel Barnes, in order to borrow £10.

The following morning Mrs Soames became ill and eventually died early on the morning of the 18 October. During this time she had been constantly nursed by Catherine. When her brother arrived later that morning he was immediately suspicious. An autopsy found nothing suspicious and at the inquest a verdict of natural death was recorded. Only a few shillings were discovered among Mrs Soames's effects and Catherine produced an IOU for £10 which paid by the relatives.

Mrs Ann Atkinson, the aunt of Catherine's dead lover, James Dixon, visited her in 1859 in her London lodgings. Mrs Atkinson ran a millinery business in Kirkby Lonsdale, and came to London annually to pay her accounts and take home more furbelows. After the two women had visited Saint Paul's, Mrs Atkinson discovered that her purse containing £51 had disappeared. In 1860 Mrs Atkinson visited Catherine again on her annual trip to London and a few day's later her husband received a telegram, 'Come at once. Wife seriously ill.' When he reached London he found his wife very ill, and she died the following day, 19th October.

Catherine told Mr Atkinson that his wife had been robbed of most of her money on Rugby Station platform and that she had had to lend her money. Atkinson repaid the alleged loan.

One Taylor with whom Catherine had been living in Lambeth left her some months later after an illness. Catherine said that he had

stolen all her money and furniture.

By 1862 Catherine had become a nurse to Mrs Sarah Carnell who was separated from her husband and wanted to be reconciled with him before her death. Catherine persuaded Carnell to return home, and his wife was so pleased that she promised to remember Catherine in her will. On the 13th of February Mrs Carnell was feeling unwell and asked Catherine to get her some medicine. The old lady became very ill after taking the medicine and Catherine disappeared. She was arrested six weeks later and charged with attempted murder and tried in the late spring at the Old Bailey. Her defence was that the fifteen-year-old boy who had served her at the chemist's had given her sulphuric acid by mistake and she was acquitted but immediately re-arrested and charged with murder. Investigations had started when a young woman, Sarah Soames, recognised the accused as the woman who had nursed her mother six years before.

Catherine was sentenced to death at the Old Bailey on 25 September 1862 for the murder of Maria Soames. Medical evidence had been given that all Mrs Soames's symptoms were consistent with poisoning by large doses of colchicum, although no trace of poison had been found at the second autopsy.

The number of murders committed by Catherine is uncertain. She was only indicted for murdering Maria Soames and Ann Atkinson, although tried on only the former charge. She was suspected of murdering Peter Mawer and James Dixon but these cases were not mentioned at the trial. She was also suspected of the murder of a Mrs Jackson of Boston who was visited frequently by Catherine in 1859. This lady drew £120 from the bank and died four days later. The money was never found. The jury must have known of these cases. No poison was found in the exhumed corpses of Mawer and Mrs Atkinson.

The death sentence was carried out on 20 October 1862 and Catherine was the last woman to be publicly hung in London.

SOURCES
Lincoln, Rutland and Stamford Mercury 3 October 1862
24 October 1862

Catherine Mary WILSON

Museum Director

Catherine Mary Bowyer was born close by Windsor Castle on 10 April 1945 and her early education was at the County Grammar School in Windsor. She developed an early interest in history and at the age of fifteen she decided to follow a museum career. Characteristically Catherine decided not to go to University and in 1964 she was successful in obtaining a post as a Museum and Gallery Assistant with Lincoln City Council and worked at the City and County Museum and Usher Gallery.

In 1968 she married Peter Wilson who was a Senior Technician with the North Lincolnshire Health Authority and is now a freelance natural history photographer. Their home is at Reepham just outside Lincoln.

Although her first interest was in archaeology Catherine became more and more interested in local history and industrial archaeology. This interest stood her in good stead when, in 1972, she was appointed Curator of the Museum of Lincolnshire Life. Catherine is particular proud of her involvement in the development of the Museum's 'outpost' at Skegness. Church Farm was a derelict site when the County Council took it over in 1976, but under Catherine's leadership it has become one of the most interesting small museums in the county.

In 1983 Catherine was appointed Assistant Director of Recreational Services for Lincolnshire County Council with responsibility for some ten Museums, art galleries and windmills. She also had overall responsibility for archaeology.

Catherine has always worked closely with voluntary organisations in the county and has had a long involvement with many heritage groups in Lincolnshire. Amongst these, she is a vice-president of the Society for Lincolnshire History and Archaeology and an Honorary Member of the Lincolnshire Mills Group. She is a honorary life member of the Friends of Heckington Windmill and of the Friends of Gainsborough Old Hall. She was also *Custos Thesauri* at Lincoln Cathedral!

Catherine has also been closely involved with museums nationally and is currently a Commissioner with the Museums and Galleries Commission (the Government's advisory body), a Board Member of the Museums Training Institute and a Council Member of the Association of Independent Museums.

Making the past relevant and enjoyable to everybody is Catherine's main interest and she particularly enjoys practical aspects of museum work and demonstrations. She was often seen either at Church Farm, Lincolnshire Life Museum or elsewhere making corn dollies, modelling Victorian costume, working windmills, driving steam engines or piloting a sailing boat on the Humber! She also had a regular

fortnightly slot on Radio Lincolnshire during which she was able to draw attention of Yellowbellys to many aspects of their heritage which might not otherwise have come to their notice.

In 1982 she was elected a Fellow of the Museums Association and in 1990 to Fellowship of the Society of Antiquaries.

In 1991 Catherine was appointed Director of the Norfolk Museums Service. Understandably, as she has involved herself in the history of Lincolnshire to an extent far beyond that required by her work, she has maintained her links (and home) in the county. She took early retirement from the Norfolk Museums Service in 1998 and is now devoting her time to museums issues nationally.

Catherine Wilson has brought a unique and enthusiastic attitude to her work in promoting public interest in the heritage of Lincolnshire and Norfolk and this was recognised nationally when, in 1996, she was appointed an Officer of the British Empire.

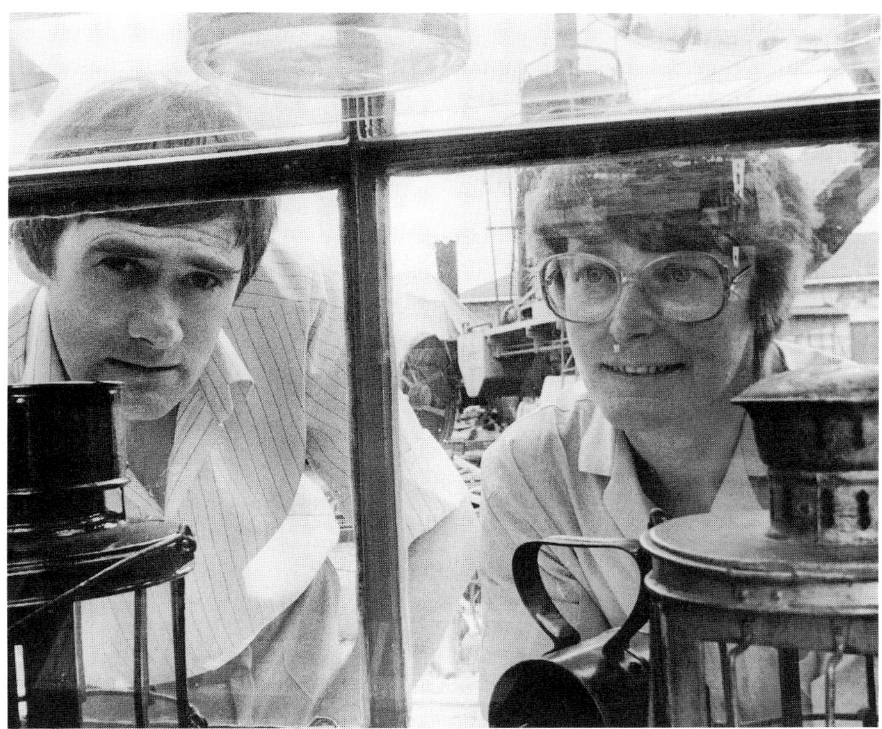

Copyright Lincolnshire Echo

Margaret WINTRINGHAM

Member of Parliament

Margaret Longbottom married Thomas Wintringham of Little Grimsby Hall in 1903. She was a native of Keighley, Yorkshire and had been educated at the Girl's Grammar School in that town. After her marriage she became a head-mistress in Grimsby. Her husband was elected the independent Liberal Member of Parliament for Louth and when he died in 1921 his widow Margaret decided to stand at the by-election.

In deference to her husband's memory she did not canvass but still won the seat and thus became the first native-born woman Member of Parliament. She was very popular and increased her majority at the election in 1923 but was defeated at the election in October 1924. Mrs Wintringham contested the Louth seat again in 1929 and the Anglesey seat in 1935 but was unsuccessful on both occasions.

During the first World War Margaret Wintringham served in the Voluntary Air Detachment. She also chaired the Woman's War Agricultural Committee. After the war she remained in public service as a magistrate and also served on the Grimsby Education Committee and Lincolnshire Agricultural Committee. She represented Caistor on Lindsey County Council from 1933 until 1945 and died on 10 March 1955.

Elizabeth WORDSWORTH

Educationalist

Elizabeth Wordsworth's association with Lincolnshire is through her father who was Bishop of Lincoln from 1869 until his death in 1884. Elizabeth was actually born in Harrow on 22 June 1840 and was the eldest of the seven children of Christopher and Susannah Wordsworth. Her father was, at that time, headmaster of Harrow School. In 1844 Christopher Wordsworth was appointed to a canonry of Westminster and in 1851 he was also appointed vicar of Stanford-in-the-Vale so Elizabeth's early life was spent either at their London home in Little Cloister, Westminster or in Berkshire.

Except for one year at a Brighton boarding school, Elizabeth's education was conducted by her father and by a succession of ladies who taught her the classics, history, English, modern languages and music. She travelled extensively and, because her father spoke openly with his children as equals, she was able to take part in discussions in London, Cambridge and Oxford devoted to scholarship, art and other matters.

Elizabeth acted as her father's secretary after he became Bishop of Lincoln and she made the residence at Riseholme her home. After the bishop died she moved to a house in Pottergate in Lincoln with her sister, Dora, and their old nurse, Janet McCraw.

In 1878 Elizabeth was appointed the first principal of Lady Margaret Hall, Oxford and here she found her lifework. During her thirty years as principal the number of students increased from nine to fifty-nine and in the university at large her personality and outlook enabled her to reconcile the more conservative elements with those who supported the higher education of women. Her common sense did much to achieve their eventual admission to the university. However, she was no feminist and her ideal was that men and women should stand equally side by side following her father's belief in their equality as human beings.

In 1886 she founded St Hugh's Hall (later St Hugh's College) in memory of her father for, as she said, 'half-a-dozen really poor students'. In 1897 she encouraged the opening of the Lady Margaret Hall Settlement for social service in Lambeth.

In 1899 that Elizabeth gave up her house in Lincoln to take up residence permanently in Oxford and she lived in that city for the remainder of her life.

Elizabeth retired in 1909 but it was not until May 1920 that Oxford University was at last able to admit women to full membership and her work was recognised by the award of an MA *honoris causa* in the following year. This seems to have caused her some amusement as she

remarked in a letter 'It is not of the smallest use to me, at my time of life... but I thought it would be ungracious to refuse...Dr Godley, the Public Orator,... will be able to poke any amount of fun at me in Latin.'

In 1926 she was elected an honorary fellow of both Lady Margaret Hall and St. Hugh's College. In 1928 in celebration of the jubilee of Lady Margaret Hall Elizabeth was awarded the honorary degree of Doctor of Civil Law and was also appointed a Dame of the British Empire.

On 3 July 1911 Elizabeth Wordsworth returned to Lincoln to open the 'New Buildings' at the Girls' High School. The work included a new wing on the left of the hall and the gymnasium and she was given a key to carry out the opening ceremony by William Watkins the architect. In her speech she compared the mystery of the working of a key with the power and influence of women's work saying "The power of a woman is a hidden power". She made an oblique reference to the suffrage and went on to say "In order to get the best out of a woman, she must be trained".

Dame Elizabeth Wordsworth gave her life to the education of women. Her wit and wisdom and, above all, her personality, did much to reconcile Oxford opinion to the admittance of women to university membership.

Under the pseudonym Grant Lloyd she published a novel, *Thornwall Abbas* in 1876 and in 1883 another novel, *Ebb and Flow*, appeared under the same pseudonym. In 1889 she published *Thoughts for the Chimney Corner; Illustrations of the Creed* followed in 1893 by *Illustrations of the Decalogue. St Christopher and Other Poems* appeared in 1890 and *Onward Steps* in 1911. In 1912 she published *Glimpses of the Past* followed in 1919 by *Essays Old and New* but her most important publication was the biography of her father written in collaboration with J. H. Overton which appeared in 1888.

This quite remarkable lady died on 30 November 1932.

FURTHER READING

Battiscombe, Georgina *Reluctant Pioneer : The life of Elizabeth Wordsworth* (1978)